WHERE NO CAR HAS GONE BEFORE

Most people in the civilized world are familiar with the Star Trek series created by the legendary Gene Roddenberry. There were the various television series, such as Star Trek: The Original Series; Star Trek: The Next Generation; Star Trek: Deep Space Nine; Star Trek: Voyager and Star Trek: Enterprise. Then there were feature films, animated episodes and hundreds of thousands of items, such as dollars, models and almost anything that has ever been seen on any Star Trek show.

What most people do not know is that there also exists a unique Star Trek car, named **Sevenuvnine**. The saga of how the Star Trek car came about is not just the story of the car, but it is more importantly, the story of how one man overcame adversity to create his dream. This is the story of how an ordinary man achieved the impossible dream. It is the story of Star Trek brought to life.

So, whether the reader is a Star Trek fan or not, this is a story that captures not only the mind, but the heart and the soul of the reader as the story of achieving the impossible dream unfolds within these pages.

This is truly a story of a drab car that became a swan, its' hidden beauty brought out by the love of one man. This car has truthfully gone where no car has gone before.

WHERE NO CAR HAS EVER GONE BEFORE!:

ACHIEVING THE IMPOSSIBLE DREAM

**BY JOHN MERCER
AS TOLD TO
KEN HUDNALL**

OMEGA PRESS

EL PASO, TEXAS

<u>Other Works By Ken Hudnall</u>

<u>The Manhattan Conspiracy Series</u>
Blood On The Apple
Capital Crimes
Angel of Death
Confrontation

<u>The Darkness Series</u>
When Darkness Falls
Fear The Darkness

<u>The Occult Connection Series</u>
UFO's, Secret Societies, and Ancient Gods

The Hidden Race

<u>The Spirits of the Border Series:</u>

The History and Mystery of El Paso Del Norte

The History and Mystery of Fort Bliss, Texas

<u>The Estate Sale Murders Series:</u>

Deadman's Diary

COPYRIGHT © 2004 Robert K. Hudnall

For permission, the writer can be contacted at:

http://www.kenhudnall.com

or through the publisher at:

http://www.omegapress.us

Written requests can be sent to:

Ken Hudnall
C/o Omega Press
5823 N. Mesa, #823
El Paso, Texas 79912

ISBN Number:

First Edition

TABLE OF CONTENTS

Figure 1: Always Expect The Unexpected!

DEDICATION

At this request of John Mercer, this book is respectfully dedicated to the woman that raised him and made him the man he is today: Vickie Mercer, his stepmother and a lady known to all as Momma Vickie. She was called home before she had a chance to see **Sevenuvnine**, her grandchild so to speak, come into her own.

You are missed!

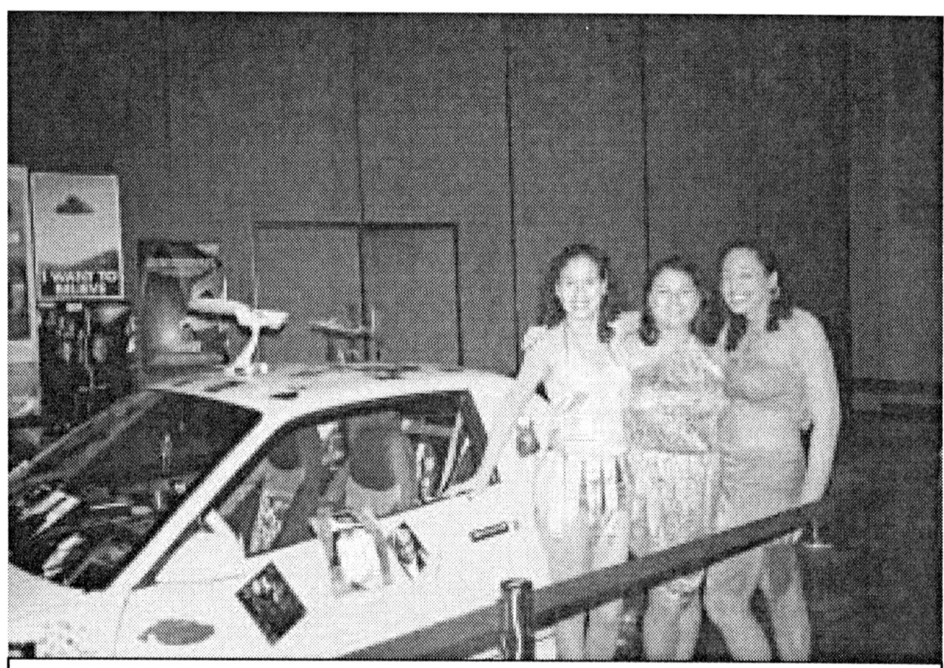

Figure 2: Sevenuvnine attracts fans from the most unusual places.

SPECIAL THANKS

There are a number of special people without whom the story of Sevenuvnine would have had a very different ending. It is only right and proper that they be mentioned in this fashion to set them apart, so to speak. The contributions of these people were so tremendous, that there is no other logical way to emphasize just how truly necessary to the successful conclusion of the project to create a Star Trek Car these people actually were. It can safely be said that without them and their big hearts, Sevenuvnine would have been stillborn.

There was John Harper, owner of StarBase 21. Without his support and friendship, there would have been no Sevenuvnine. There is James Harper who was so behind the concept of creating the Star Trek Car that he gave up his breaks and worked StarBase 21 so that John Harper would work with John Mercer to handle things.

There was the one and only Chris Dunavan who helped create Sevenuvnine's website and who gave uncompromising support to Sevenuvnine on her long road to reach where she is today.

There is Raymond Anders who sometimes forgets to turn off his stupid chip, but who had given his full support to projects of all type.

Josh Hess doesn't really know what Star Trek is except for what his dad knows, but he totally supports the car all the same.

Then of course, we cannot forget Engle, who trailers the car wherever it needs to go, usually at his own expense and who donated the eleven Star Trek Bears to Sevenuvnine.

However, the contributions of all of the others would have been for naught if not for the outstanding, wholehearted love and support shown by John's wife, Trish Mercer. This little lady has the patience of a Saint and a love beyond all calculation. If John Mercer is Sevenuvnine's father, then Trish is certainly Sevenuvnine's mother. Without her support and understanding, John would not have been able to invest the $80,000.00 plus dollars that has gone into Sevenuvnine over the last five years.

There is a special thanks that must go out to all of the support staff at the many Star Trek Conventions that John has attended with Sevenuvnine that went out of their way to help him get the many autographs that now adorn the body of the one and only Star Trek Car. These people donate their time and efforts to help make the shows happen out of the sheer love of Star Trek and without any rewards other than knowing that they have brought joy and excitement to the fans and their communities.

Thanks to the USS Celt, our Ship in StarFleet Command, and the crew Ray Harper, Jan Blaylock, Shawn Boyd, Mark Blaylock, Carmen Schultz, Jason Staats, Larry Roberts, Brian Roberts, and Nathan Marcy. And to my best buddy, Jason Williamson.

Finally, last but certainly not least, there is a tremendous thanks that must go out to all of the fans that have supported Sevenuvnine; who have donated various items to be added to the car and who have sent pictures that they have taken of various stars signing the car. You are the reason that all of this is done.

John Mercer
Fayetteville, Arkansas
2004

Ken Hudnall
El Paso, Texas
2004

Figure 3: Eugene Wesley Roddenberry

Figure 4: John Mercer and Sevenuvnine, The Star Trek Car

CHAPTER ONE

MORE THAN A TELEVISION SHOW

In November 21, 2003, John Mercer, the owner of one of the most unusual cars in the world undertook to tell the story of the creation of what has become known as the one and only Star Trek Car. While the story of the creation of this unique symbol of the Star Trek phenomenon is certainly interesting in and of itself, I think the more intriguing story is how the creation of a simple television show has had such an unbelievable impact on the public consciousness around the world. No matter what the country, no matter what the language, there is hardly a soul that does not understand the phrase *"Beam Me Up Scotty."* It is absolutely unbelievable that a production, with very few of the sophisticated special effects audiences have come to expect today has become such an identifiable part of society.

However, before continuing with this narrative regarding the creation of a unique symbol for a television and movie series, I think it only right to give a little history of Star Trek from its inception for those of you who may have lived under a rock for the last forty or so years. Few people seem to realize that there were actually two different incarnations of the original Star Trek television show.

Figure 5: Jeffrey Hunter (Photo From Writer's Collection)

The first pilot for the series[1] had the Starship Enterprise being commanded by Captain Christopher Pike, portrayed by Jeffrey Hunter, a fairly well known Hollywood leading man with actress Majel Barrett, the future Mrs. Gene Roddenberry[2], as his first officer and Leonard Nimoy as the Vulcan science officer, Spock. Unfortunately for Gene Roddenberry, but fortunately for millions of Star Trek fans around the world, even though the story of ***The Cage*** received outstanding critical reviews, and it cost the studio $630,000.00[3] to make, the original pilot was not well received by the decision makers at NBC, in fact, they thought that the episode was too cerebral and lacking action and adventure. The studio bosses also objected to a female second in command, feeling that the public would never accept this concept. Finally, they definitely did not like the "guy with the pointed ears!" because it was felt that his demonic appearance would offend any number of religious groups. However, they did like the first pilot well enough and so a second pilot was ordered.

---

[1] The first pilot episode aired in 1965 and was called The Cage. See Appendix A for a full list of cast members.

[2] Eugene Wesley Roddenberry and Majel Barrett were married on August 6, 1969.

[3] At the time The Cage was produced, the $630,000.00 price tag made it the most expensive pilot ever produced.

One hurtle that had to be overcome before this second pilot could be filmed was the replacement of the lead actor in the series. Jeffrey Hunter[4], Captain Christopher Pike, decided not to return and continue the series. The reason given to the public was that he wished to work on feature films rather than continue to do a television series. However, insiders reported that Hunter's wife had made such had been outrageous demands on Roddenberry than it was Gene Roddenberry who decided to replace Hunter. Whatever the reason, the second pilot stared a new captain[5].

The new captain of the USS Enterprise was a young actor by the name of William Shatner. Shatner, as Captain James T. Kirk, along with Leonard Nimoy, who reprised his role as the half Vulcan, half human Spock, James Doohan as Chief Engineer Scott and Deforest Kelly as Doctor Leonard H. McCoy, explored the galaxy for three seasons until, in 1969, its third season, NBC cancelled the show[6]. As far as the network chiefs felt, the show had gone about as far as it could go and it was time to pull the plug.

The reasons for the cancellation were many. In spite of the series' critical acclaim, NBC had never been happy with the ratings. In fact there had been two earlier attempts to cancel the series that were averted by letter writing campaigns by fans. Gene Roddenberry had been promised that for the third season, the show would be slotted for 7:30 Monday night, prime time, but at the last minute, the network broke its promise and slotted the show was in a 10:00 pm Friday night time slot, which virtually guaranteed extremely low ratings and eventual cancellation at the same time it cut the production budget. Gene Roddenberry's response to this move on the part of the network was to resign from the series that he had created. The lack of funding and the loss of the creative genius that had given birth to Star Trek were two hurdles that the show could not overcome and the final episode, entitled ***"Turnabout Intruder"*** aired a mere six weeks before man first set foot on the Moon.

---

[4] It is an interesting aside that Jeffrey Hunter later died in somewhat mysterious circumstances.

[5] In this second pilot, entitled *"Where No Man Has Gone Before,"* Roddenberry removed the female second in command as NBC directed, but he insisted on keeping Spock with his demonic appearance. In fact, Spock was the only character from the first pilot to appear in the second pilot. This second pilot was shot in eight days and only cost $330,000.00. Majel Barrett later returned as Nurse Chapel on Star Trek, the original series.

[6] The original series was cancelled on June 3, 1969.

This cancellation came as something of a surprise to the millions of fans of this ground breaking series, as it had recently even received critical acclaim, having been nominated for and winning two Hugo Awards during its three season run. In 1967, Star Trek was nominated for its first Hugo Award and won for Best Dramatic Presentation for the episode The Menagerie and again in 1968 it was nominated for and won for Best Dramatic Presentation for the episode entitled The City on the Edge of Forever.

However, the attitude of NBC shows just how wrong the so-called experts can be about what the public wants to see. The show had touched a nerve in the public psyche, suddenly fans demanded to see more of the adventures of the crew of the Enterprise. Instead of fading away as most fans clubs of cancelled television shows have the tendency to do, the Star Trek fan clubs grew in size and sophistication. The fan clubs celebrated not the career of a particular star on the show, but rather the concept that the human race is not alone in the universe. Star Trek Conventions began to be held around the country with the first one being held in January 1972. At first these conventions were small, attended by only the most die-hard fans. However, soon, these events began to draw crowds that numbered in the thousands. A new phenomenon was born.

Responding to the unbelievable demand for the cancelled series, in September 1973, Star Trek: The Animated Series aired. This animated version was not the fan favorite that the original series had been, however, because it ended in October of 1974, having lasted only a little more than a year. During the latter part of the 1970s, a new Star Trek Show was put into development, however, with the release of Star Wars, the idea of a new incarnation of Star Trek was shelved. Instead the pilot for the new series was rewritten as a movie for release on the big screen. This movie, released in 1979 by Paramount Pictures and staring most of the original cast, was entitled ***Star Trek: The Motion Picture***.

To the surprise of the network brass that had cancelled the original series, the release of the movie proved that there was a growing demand for more Star Trek adventures. The movie was a major hit and public interest was shown to be as high as ever. Deciding to capitalize on this stunning discovery, the studio released five more movies using the original cast throughout the 1980s and the early 1990s.

In 1982, Paramount released ***Star Trek II: The Wrath of Khan***, drawing its story line from one of the episodes of the original series that starred Ricardo Montalban. This new movie picked up the story where the series left off. Most of the original cast reprised their original roles. This movie also saw the death of a fan favorite as Mr. Spock died saving the rest of the crew of the Enterprise. In spite the end of Spock, the fans loved this second feature movie and money poured into the Paramount coffers.

In 1984, Paramount released ***Star Trek III: The Search For Spock***. In this movie, the perennial goods guys highjack a star ship and go forth looking for the deceased Mr. Spock. The writers experimented with resurrecting a killed off main character in a completely believable manner. The fans clubs clamored for more and the movie going public flocked to the theater as a new generation of fans discovered the wonders of Star Trek.

In 1986, Paramount released ***Star Trek IV: The Voyage Home***. In this installment, Kirk and his closest companions, along with the resurrected Mr. Spock once again save the universe from the bad guys and then have to answer for their crimes against the Federation. The end result opens the doors for many more Star Trek movies with former Admiral, now reduced to Captain James T. Kirk sitting in the commander's chair. Once again, the fans of Captain Kirk literally threw their money at the box office.

In 1989, Paramount released ***Star Trek V: The Final Frontier***, dealing with the concept of peace between the Federation and the Klingons. This was, of course, a mirroring of the pending collapse of the Soviet Empire, much as the Klingon Empire began to fall to its knees, having over spent on their war like preparations, bankrupting their society. Whatever it may have been based upon, the fans loved it.

Then on December 6, 1991, the last of the original Star Trek movies, ***Star Trek VI: The Undiscovered Country***, was released to a space hungry audience. This film delved into the concept of New Agers looking for God that had its beginning in one of the original episodes from the original series.

The year 1987 saw the release of a new television series entitled ***Star Trek: The Next Generation***. This new show, featuring Patrick Stewart as Captain Jean-Luc Picard, Jonathan Frakes as Executive Officer, Commander William T. Riker, Michael Dorn as the Klingon Worf, Brent Spiner as the android, Data, and Gates McFadden as Doctor Beverly Crusher was a gamble since the original cast would appear only sporadically and then only for a few shows. No one could predict how the public would react to these new heroes of the space ways. However, the fans of the original Star Trek had begun to give away to the next generation of viewers, the new show was greeted with open arms by fans of the original show and new fans alike, it lasted for seven seasons, from 1987 to May of 1994[7].

The seed that Gene Roddenberry planted with his futuristic vision of space exploration was beginning to grow and spread. From the initial series, which looks dated to those who grew up with Star Wars type special effects, an entire universe of shows began to spring forth, taking the human imagination to places not even dreamed of in 1966.

On January 2, 1992, ***Star Trek: Deep Space Nine*** previewed to an expectant audience. This series was filmed primarily aboard a once Cardassian owned space station that was now the property of the Federation. Avery Brooks starred as Captain Benjamin Lafayette Sisko, the first Black actor to be both Commander and a major character in the weekly story line. This series lasted six seasons before leaving the air. However, this first, non-USS Enterprise space series showed that the public shared Gene Roddenberry's dream of leaving the bounds of earth and soaring into the heavens in search of other adventures and other races. This series ended June 2, 1999[8].

---

[7] ***Star Trek: The Next Generation*** was also a critically acclaimed series. In 1990, the series was nominated for an Emmy Award for Outstanding Sound Mixing for a Drama Series for the episode "Yesterday's Enterprise." In 1992, the series was again nominated for an Emmy Award, and won, for Outstanding Individual Achievement in Special Visual Effects for the episode entitled "The Condrum." Then in 1994, the series received its third Emmy nomination for Outstanding Drama Series.

In 1993, the series was nominated and won a Hugo Award for Best Dramatic Presentation for the episode "The Inner Light."

In 1995 Patrick Stewart was nominated or a Screen Actor Guild Award for Outstanding Performance by a Male Actor in a Drama Series.

In 1988 Wil Wheaton, who portrayed Wesley Crusher on the series, was nominated for a Young Artist Award as Best Young Actor Starring in a Television Series. In 1989, the series was nominated for a Young Artist Award and won for Best Syndicated Family Drama or Comedy Series. In 1989, Wil Wheaton was nominated for a Young Artist Award and won for Best Young Actor in a family Syndicated Show. In 1990 the series was nominated for a Young Artist Award for Best Off-Primetime Family Series. In 1990 Wil Wheaton was nominated for a Young Artist Award for Best Young Actor in an Off-Primetime Family Series.

[8] Like its predecessors, ***Star Trek: Deep Space Nine*** also won or was nominated for several important awards during its run. In 1998, the series was nominated for and won the ASCAP Film and Television Award for Top TV Series. In 1999, the series was nominated by the Academy of Science Fiction, Horror and Fantasy Films for Best Genre Cable/Syndicated Nominated Series.

In 1995, the series was nominated by the American Society of Cinematographers for Outstanding Achievement in Cinematography in Regular Series (Crossover).

In 1994, ***Star Trek: Generations***, the seventh movie based upon the Star Trek phenomenon premiered. An imaginative and unusual plot twist in the story line allowed the use of crew members from both the original series as well as The Next Generation. In this movie, the writers did something that usually sounds the death knell for a series, no matter how well received it may originally appear. After hundreds of adventures, the writers finally allowed the seemingly immortal Captain James T. Kirk to die and the U.S.S. Enterprise itself to be destroyed in battle. However such is the resilience of this series the even the death of so beloved a character as Kirk only added a new level of interest as fans waited to see how, and if, he will be brought back to life, for in space, all things are possible.

In 1995, ***Star Trek: Voyager,*** a new television series based on Gene Roddenberry's dreams of space exploration, was released by the new United Paramount Network. The series lasted approximately six

---

In 1995, the series won an Emmy Award for Outstanding Individual Achievement in Makeup for a Series and was nominated for Outstanding Individual Achievement in Special Visual Effects for the episode entitled The Jem'Hadar and for Outstanding Individual Achievement in Hairstyling for a Series for the episode entitled Improbable Cause. In 1996, the series was nominated for Emmy Awards in the following categories: Outstanding Individual Achievement in Costume Design for a Series for the episode entitled The Muse; Outstanding Individual Achievement in Hairstyling for a Series for the episode entitled Our Man Bashir; Outstanding Individual Achievement in Makeup for a Series for the episode entitled The Visitor; Outstanding Individual Achievement in Music Composition for a Series for the episode entitled Our Man Bashir; Outstanding Individual Achievement in Special Visual Effects for the episode entitled The Way of the Warrior. In 1997, the series was nominated for the following Emmy Awards: Outstanding Individual Achievement in Art Direction for a Series for the episode entitled Trials and Tribbleations; Outstanding Individual Achievement in Cinematography for a Series for the episode entitled Apocalypse Rising; Outstanding Individual Achievement in Hairstyling for a Series for the Episode entitled Trials and Tribbleations; and Outstanding Special Visual Effects for the episode entitled Trials and Tribbleations. In 1999, the series was nominated for Emmy Awards for: Outstanding Art Direction for a Series for an episode entitled Prodigal Daughter; Outstanding Hairstyling for a Series for the episode entitled Badda-Bing Badda-Bang; and Outstanding Makeup for a Series for an episode entitled Dogs of War.

In 1996, the series was nominated for a Hugo Award for Best Dramatic Presentation for an episode entitled The Visitor. The series was also nominated in 1997 for Best Dramatic presentation.

In 1996 and 1997, star Avery Brooks was nominated for Image Awards for Outstanding Lead Actor in a Drama Series. In 1998, the series won an International Monitor Award for Film Originated Television Series for Electronic Visual Effects for an episode entitled Call To Arms. Finally, in 1997, cast member Cirroc Lofton was nominated for a Young Star Award for Best Performance by a Young Actor in a Drama Series

seasons before it too flew its last mission on May 23, 2001[9]. However, in its numerous adventures, Voyager added a number of new characters to the Star Trek legend.

In 1996, Paramount needed a hit movie and the legions of loyal fans needed another Star Trek fix; so a new Star Trek movie entitled ***Star Trek: First Contact*** was released by Paramount Pictures. This movie moved the basic "space western" onto a new level with stunning special effects and time travel thrown in for good measure. It also allowed fans to see some of the history incorporated into the Star Trek storyline.

In 1998, ***Star Trek: Insurrection*** premiered on the big screen. This plot featured an alien race fighting to retain control of their planet and hiding a secret that could throw the universe into total confusion.

In 1999, Star Trek received an honor that very few other works of fiction have ever received. The United States Post Office issued the new Star Trek Stamp. Naturally, fans bought those stamps like they were going out of style.

With the long track record of fans wanting anything Star Trek, on September 26, 2001, a new action/adventure television series based upon the continuing exploits of a crew aboard an earlier star ship was released by United Paramount Network (UPN). This new series was the first one not to carry the Star Trek name in its title, being called simply ***Enterprise***. This series dealt with a period of time 100 years before the original Star Trek series. However, this series was not very well received so the name was changed to Star Trek: Enterprise and ratings improved.

On December 13, 2002, a new movie, ***Star Trek: Nemesis***, was released for the big screen. For the first time since the original series was cancelled, a Star Trek offering was a failure; at least in the mind of the pencil pushers at the studio, it did not live up to expectations. The movie took in lass than $50 million dollars at the Box Office. Of course, most movies would be ecstatic to earn in the neighborhood of $50 million dollars in the United States, but the producers of the Star Trek movies were accustomed to earning far more than this paltry sum.

In addition to the movies and television series that have sprouted from the seeds planted by Gene Roddenberry, there have been tens of thousands of actions figures, trading cards, toys, clothing, games and literally hundreds of titles chronicling the adventures of the Enterprise and

---

[9] The Awards won by this series are too numerous to mention here, but please check the Appendices in the back of the book for a great deal of other information regarding these accomplishments.

the Federation. These hundreds of titles have sold millions of copies around the globe. The sheer number of Star Trek related titles could fill a small library all by itself. I can not think of another show that has gone on to hold such a place in the hearts and minds of millions of people, extending across races, genders, creeds and even generations. It is truly one of the most unbelievable stories in the history of television.

The actors who portrayed the lead characters in the original Star Trek series have achieved a level of acclaim that most major motion picture stars can only aspire to achieve. The following individuals who have been associated with Star Trek phenomenon have been honored by receiving a Star on the Hollywood Walk of Fame, one of the highest honors that can be given to an actor by the town that was built on dreams.

*May 19, 1983 William Shatner, more familiarly known to millions of fans as Captain James T. Kirk;

*January 16, 1985, Leonard Nimoy, better known as Mr. Spock;

*September 4, 1985, the creator of the Star Trek series, Gene Roddenberry received his Star[10];

*October 30, 1986, George Takei, better known as Mr. Sulu;

*November 15, 1990, LeVar Burton, better known as Commander Geordi LaForge;

*December 18, 1991, Deforest Kelly, who portrayed Dr. Leonard McCoy, received his honor[11];

*January 9, 1992, Nichelle Nichols, one of the first African American females to be offered a featured role during the 1960s portrayed Communications Officer Lieutenant Uhura, received her star.

Gene Roddenberry had successfully created a completely new universe, populated it with believable characters and touched a part of the human spirit that most Hollywood writers do not realize even exist. It is this aspect of what many looked at as just another television show that led John Mercer down his own personal path toward enlightenment and gave him his own personal goal in life.

However, even the most optimistic fan could never have predicted how deeply a mere television show had affected the viewing audience. No one has ever been able to explain the truly world wide appeal of this

---

[10] Sadly, Gene Roddenberry, the brilliant creator of this unbelievable series of shows and movies died on October 24, 1991. The Star Trek franchise is now owned by Paramount Pictures, but the Roddenberry name is still one to carry weight in Hollywood through his equally able son and heir, Gene Roddenberry, Jr.

[11] Deforest Kelly died on June 11, 1999.

series. However, perhaps in learning about the journey of John Mercer to obtain his place in the annuals of this concept that will never die will allow the reader to have some idea of what a fictional world can come to mean to real ordinary people in this world.

Join me as we learn about the birth of **Sevenuvnine**, a dream that has assumed a life all its own.

CHAPTER TWO

A MAN WITH A MISSION

In 1966, to the decision makers at NBC *Star Trek* was a science fiction show that might make money for the network, but nothing more. After all, CBS was working on a more adult science fiction series entitled *"Lost In Space"* so science fiction was becoming the new fad in the world of the small screen. However, though Lost In Space, with its larger budget was to achieve the label of a cult series, to millions of little boys across this land, Star Trek was to become a signpost pointing them toward the last frontier, a place where no man had gone before.

It is appropriate that man first walked on the Moon shortly after the cancellation of the original Star Trek series[12] as if the unbelievable achievement of a human walking on the Moon somehow underscored the visionary genius of Gene Roddenberry. After all, it was the imagination of scientists who had once been small boys who dreamed of space travel that resulted in this momentous achievement.

One of those small boys sitting in front of the television avidly following the adventures of Captain Kirk and Mr. Spock was John Mercer. I think that the journey of John Mercer from the little boy captivated in front of a black and white television screen to the man who has single

---

[12] Neil Armstrong and the Apollo 11 Crew landed on the Moon in July of 1969.

handedly made a place for himself in relation to this legendary series is representative of how the lives of the fictional Captain James T. Kirk and the rest of his crew have become important to the world at large. If nothing else, the adventures of the crew of the USS Enterprise has shown us that nothing is impossible to men and women of imagination.

How John Mercer came to this point in his life where his creation is now the subject of a book is a journey every bit as unusual and unique as that of the crew of the original U.S.S. Enterprise in the series created by Gene Roddenberry. Even more than the crew of the fictional Enterprise, whose pathway was laid out for them by the script writers, John has truly gone where no man, or car, has ever gone before and his journey is, I think, representative of what this series, on the air for only three seasons before being canceled by network "experts", has come to mean to the American psyche.

The telling of this most unusual story of one man's self-appointed mission to create a most unique symbol for the show that meant so much to him began in a very uneventful way. He received an invitation to attend the Star Trek Convention being held in El Paso, Texas. He had been to a number of Star Trek Conventions around the country, but there was something about this one that was unique. It was while he and his creation were in El Paso that he decided that is was time to tell the story of what led him to become a part of the legend that is Star Trek.

According to John Mercer, he has been involved with Star Trek most of his life, in fact, his most memorable childhood memories revolve around some phase of the Star Trek phenomenon. However, this is John's story and I will let him tell it in the way that he sees best. According to this remarkable young man, while in El Paso, he met a gentleman, an author, who inspired him to tell his story of the good times and bad, the frustrating and sad times he experienced in his campaign to create the one and only Star Trek car that he called **Sevenuvnine**[13]. To use John's own words, this is the story of a Star Trek fan that wanted to make a difference.

This unique story begins when John was ten years old. He describes his family as dysfunctional and like many individuals who have come from such backgrounds he has few distinct, specific memories of his early formative years. However, one memory that is distinct in his mind is sitting in front of a television set watching the crew of the USS Enterprise explore the galaxy and go where no man had ever gone before. He

---

[13] Sevenuvnine (Tertiary Adjunct of Unimatrix Zero-One) was the name of a half human, half Borg character played by Jeri Lynn Ryan on the series *Star Trek: Voyager*.

identified with those fictional characters who were always able to solve their problems, so matter how large or how serious they might be. Star Trek was his escape from the problems that surrounded him.

Figure 6: John Mercer with Scotty.

His fascination with the weekly television series did not go unnoticed by his elders. As parents are wont to do, when he failed to follow their many rules and regulations, he was denied his cherished *Star Trek* until they felt he had been punished enough. But sometimes even the strictest parent has a soft spot for their offspring whether it can be seen or not. The same year that he turned ten years old, he received, what was to him, the ultimate Christmas present. The memory of this present and the joy that it brought to this little boy has stayed with him long after age and use has consigned the gift to the scrap heap. This remarkable, unforgettable present was a play set containing a replica of the bridge of the USS Enterprise about the size of a monopoly board.

In his retelling of his childhood, he talked for a long time and with great feeling about the joy he received from this Star Trek toy. What came from his description of this Christmas present was the fact that it was not only the replica of a make believe starship bridge, but it was an actual bridge that brought he and his sister closer together.

John related that he had two of the earliest Star Trek action figures, Captain Kirk and Mr. Spock. He spent endless hours cruising the galaxy with his two favorite heroes, turning the buttons on his replica bridge to make the transporter energize, taking them to strange new worlds and exciting adventures far from the cares of this world and the less than joyful life of a little boy on Planet Earth.

He and his sister would also play together with this, once in a life time Christmas present, he would be the dashing Captain Kirk and she the long legged, stunning communications officer, Lieutenant Uhura[14]. In their imaginary world, they would while away the hours, putting aside their cares and losing themselves in the wonderful world of the imagination; a gift belonging to most children that is so sadly lacking in most adults.

Sometimes we lose track of our childhood dreams. When we become adults we put away the dreams that had meant so much to us, so it was with John Mercer until *Sevenuvnine* entered his life and nothing has been the same since.

---

[14] The word uhura is from the Swahili language and means freedom.

CHAPTER THREE

THE BIRTH OF SEVENUVNINE

John grew to manhood and like most adults, he was forced to put aside his dreams of childhood for his life was filled with a new set of adventures and problems. For each of us, the challenges that we face as adults cause us to put aside the fantasy world, even a fantasy world so exciting as that of Star Trek. Even so, in the back of his mind, there was always that part of him that still yearned to be a part of the world of space and the adventures of his boyhood heroes. For most of us, this is an impossible dream, but most of us do not have the drive and desire of John Mercer.

So it was that in the course of time, John decided that he wanted to build a car, but not just any car, a car that would be a rolling monument to the characters that had meant so much to him as a boy. While Star Trek h ad flown off into that unknown universe of cancelled shows, Captain Kirk and Mr. Spock still undertook adventures in the far reaches of his dreams. One day he took the step that most of us wish that we could, he decided to make his dream a reality. He decided that he wanted to build a Star Trek Car.

In 1996, John was living in Talico, Oklahoma, his dream of building the Stat Trek car still just a desire and a hope. Mystics say that some things are just meant to be and so it seems with John Mercer and the car that has come to represent his dream. In this little out of the way town, he saw an old, gray, beat up Camaro that frankly had nothing to distinguish it from any other old beat up car. The only remarkable thing was that even though the car was long past its best years it had been outfitted with souped up tires by the owner.

It is actually remarkable that John even gave the car a second glance. This car was old and tired, its best years lost in the dream world of the past. But to John Mercer this tired beat up old car struck a cord. In spite of its outer appearance, he thought that this car looked cool and, even though the car was in really terrible shape, both inside and out, he somehow knew that he had found his Star Trek Car. The desire to purchase the car, that was now only a pale ghost of the beautiful piece of machinery that it had once been, was overwhelming and before he could change his mind, he made the purchase.

Even with the car in his possession, the obstacles standing between him and his dream of building the first Star Trek car were tremendous. The car, a 1990 Chevy Z28, was a mechanical nightmare; the engine needed to be completely rebuilt and the upholstery was an embarrassment. In fact, John made the comment that the upholstery was in the worst shape of any car that he had ever seen. However, in spite of all of these negatives, he never believed for one minute that his precious car it would not become the very first Star Trek car, a monument to the dreams and determination of Gene Roddenberry. What was not mentioned and John Mercer was too self-effacing to even consider it, but the creation of the Star Trek car was also a monument to the dreams and determination of one John Mercer.

John's original purpose for creating the Star Trek car was to have a unique, cool looking car to simply drive around town. Having obtained the body of the car that he envisioned as the one and only Star Trek car, he spent hours working on the engine until he had it purring like one of Scotty's beloved engines. Now he could drive the car, but it was a long way from the powerful machine that he could envision in his dreams.

It is interesting how what we envision is not always what we wind up creating. True he wanted a Star Trek car, but in his mind, he envisioned this unique car as luminous green. His ever supportive wife, Trish, encouraged her husband to realize his dream, but urged him to paint the car bright yellow. She commented that since he loved Star Trek so much, that he should paint the car yellow to reflect the blonde hair of Jeri Lynn Ryan, one of his favorite actresses from ***Star Trek: Voyager.***

Having received "official" permission to upgrade his precious car

Figure 7: Jeri Lynn Ryan as Sevenuvnine on Star Trek: Voyager

from his own first officer, Trish, John went to the local Maaco dealer and for $600.00 he purchased their top of the line paint job. However, with typical male stubbornness, he ignored his wife's advice and had the car painted a bright green. In his own mind, he knew that this original paint job was the most hideous paint job that had ever been placed on a car, but it was all that he could afford and he certainly was not about to let anyone know of his dissatisfaction.

Proudly, he drove his newly painted car home to show his wife. Trish, with typical wifely insight into her husband's ego, made no comment on how badly the bright green paint job looked on the car, but rather she again urged him to have the car painted a bright corvette yellow to represent Jeri Lynn Ryan's hair.

He was privately so disappointed with the appearance of his car that he finally took his wife's advice and repainted his car Corvette yellow. Next he went to a local store and bought an 8 x 10 picture of actress Jeri Lynn Ryan. His original plan had been to place the photo on the hood of his car, but he decided that 8 x 10 was not a large enough sized picture for his purposes. To remedy this problem, he took the photo to a sign company and requested them to make him a full color sticker of the picture large enough to cover the entire hood of his car.

There was no doubt in his mind that the sign company technicians thought he was a little touched, but at a cost of $500.00, this sign company converted the 8 x 10 picture of Jeri Lynn Ryan into a huge sticker just the right size to cover the entire hood of his car. This massive likeness of the beautiful young actress was the first step in his ultimate plan to create a totally unique symbol of Star Trek and the future that he visualized. The next step in his plan was to obtain a distinctive tag. Though I sure that they wondered what he intended, but after the payment of the required fees, John was assigned the tag *7uv9*.

At this point in time, John stepped back to carefully consider his accomplishments to this point. We are always our own worst critics, but even John had to admit that the outside looked awesome. Unfortunately, then inside of the car was still trashed. Even so, he felt that it was time to unveil himself and his creation to the world, so he began to look for a suitable venue where the world would learn about the birth of **THE STAR TREK CAR!**

CHAPTER FOUR

THE JOURNEY BEGINS

Figure 8: The USS Enterprise A

None of us likes change, especially when it impacts something that we have come to place on a pedestal. Star Trek, which now lived only in the memories of the millions of early fans was changing. There would be a new series aired of this legendary series. This notice sent shock waves throughout the world of "believers." In 1987, *Star Trek: The Next Generation* aired. Gone were the courageous Captain Kirk, the pointy eared Mr. Spock and the crusty old Dr. McCoy. Now it was a bald Captain Picard, a mind reading ship's counselor and an android that wanted to be human. Initially John, as well as many other die-hard Trekkie fans, were totally opposed to these changes; to them, it was not Star Trek!

However, out of curiosity more than anything else, he began to follow the adventures of the new Enterprise and discovered to his surprise that he began to identify with the new characters and enjoyed their adventures as much as he had the voyages of the original starship Enterprise. New heroes began to filter into his psyche, new ideas replaced those of the original series. Finally, he decided that this new series was every bit as awesome as the original series.

One thing that the new show caused was an increase in Star Trek related events. Surprisingly enough, Tulsa, Oklahoma became a hot bed of Star Trek fans and many Star Trek events took place in this city. It was in Tulsa at a UPN network event that John Mercer decided to make the world aware of his creation. This event took place at a local club and the UPN girls were present to publicize the new series. John made the decision to begin his long journey toward public acceptance of the Star Trek Car.

At the time of this event in late 1987, his car still had the huge picture of Jeri Lynn Ryan covering the entire hood, but he wanted to show it off anyway. He called the club management and asked if he could bring the Star Trek Car in order to show it off. The sponsors of the vents had never heard about a Star Trek Car, but they figured that if he wanted to bring the car at his own expense and display it outside the club, they had nothing to lose. So John Mercer attended his first event as the proud owner of the world's first Star Trek Car.

So it was that John Mercer arrived at the club in Tulsa, OK with his Corvette yellow car, its hood covered with Jeri Lynn Ryan's picture. Like any new father, he was proud of his creation and wanted to show it off. It was at this first event that he had his first pictures taken with the Star Trek Car. The UPN girls were all fascinated by the unique car and clamored to have their pictures taken with the car and its owner. UPN photographers covering the event, who naturally flocked around the scantily clad girls, took a lot of photos and film of the girls crowded around John Mercer and his unique car.

In 1999, John became aware of the plans to hold a major Star Trek Convention in Tulsa. His excitement grew when he found out that Kate Mulgrew, who portrayed Captain Kathryn Janeway on ***Star Trek:***

Voyager, the Borg Queen[15] and some other stars from the various Star Trek series planned on being in attendance. He felt that this was his chance to begin his journey to achieving his own dream of acceptance for the Star Trek Car.

His first hurtle, of course, was how to get permission to be part of the convention.

Figure 9: Kate Mulgrew (Captain Kathyn Janeway) from Star Trek:Voyager

He made some calls and discovered that John Harper, owner of a company called StarBase 21[16], was going to be the primary sponsor of the upcoming event. John had never met John Harper, but that didn't stop him. Gathering his nerve, John called John Harper and asked if he and his car could be part of the show in order to place the Star Trek Car on display.

---

[15] This role was originated by Alice Krige in the 1996 film, *Star Trek: First Contact*, but when the character became part of the *Star Trek: Voyager* series, Alice Krige was not available and the role was played by a new actress, Susanna Thompson.

[16] Starbase 21, Inc. is located at 2130 South Sheridan Road, Tulsa, OK 74129-1002. (918) 838-3388. Website is http://www.starbase21ok.com. This is one of the most complete retail stores in the country featuring comics, games, sports and CCG Cards, T-Shirts, Posters, Action Figures, CDs, Star Trek, Star Wars, Babylon 5, and SCI-Fi Collectibles.

John Mercer wasn't sure what type of response he actually expected from John Harper, but to his utter surprise, John Harper was quite agreeable to John bringing the Star Trek Car; he just asked that UPN, Channel 41, agree to sponsor the entry of the Car. Unable to believe this unexpected luck, John immediately called UPN 41 and obtained their agreement to sponsor his entry into the Star Trek Convention. He was all set to take part in his very first Convention; the first step in achieving his dream of having the very first Star Trek Car.

Now that he had permission to be part of the Convention, he had to get everything ready. He wanted to put Kate Mulgrew's picture on the hood of the car, but there was no room, as the huge picture of Jeri Lynn Ryan covered the entire hood. Finally, he decided to take the huge hood covering Jeri Lynn Ryan picture and reduced it back down to 11" x 10". Then he put Kate Mulgrew's picture on the right side of Jeri Lynn Ryan's picture and a photo of the Borg Queen on the left side.

With high expectations, he went to this first convention with his car with only 3 pictures on the hood of the car and absolutely no autographs. This first convention began on a Friday afternoon and John was almost quivering with excitement. However, those who attended this first convention came to see the stars of their favorite series, not a car belonging to an unknown individual, located all the way in the back of the auditorium with three pictures on its hood. There was no question that the car was a beautiful machine, but there was nothing special about it as far as most of those in attendance were concerned.

John had worked long and hard to turn Sevenuvnine into a work of art and he was proud of how the outside looked. Naturally, he had neither the time nor the money to do much about the inside so he kept the windows up and made sure not to open the doors. However, in spite of the beauty of his creation, to his disappointment he, and the one and only Star Trek car, **Sevenuvnine,** were ignored by all.

Figure 10: Denise Crosby

Finally, deciding that he had to do something to gain some attention for his car, he gathered up his courage and approached Denise Crosby, the lovely young actress that played Lieutenant Tasha Yar, the security chief on *Star Trek: The Next Generation.* After some initial conversation, he asked her if she would agree to autograph his car and to his amazement, she agreed without hesitation.

John Mercer was the proudest man at the show as he escorted Denise Crosby back to the rear of the auditorium where **Sevenuvnine** sat quietly, over looked by most of those in attendance. He stood beside her as the lovely Denise Crosby placed her autograph on the shiny yellow surface of **Sevenuvnine**. He felt that he was on the way to achieving his dream. Unfortunately, after this first success, there was some resistance to his plan of having each star at the Convention sign his car. Some of them seemed to feel that it was absolutely ridiculous, and somehow beneath them, to sign a car and refused to do so.

The Star Trek Convention in Tulsa, Oklahoma promoted by John Harper's StarBase 21, is always a 3 day convention. So on Saturday, the second day of this first show, John continued his campaign to meet each star in attendance and ask them to sign his automobile. Saturday, he continued to meet other stars and he politely asked each one of them to sign his car. To his delight, The Borg Queen seemed fascinated by the idea of a car dedicated to the Star Trek phenomenon and she became the second star to sign the gleaming **Sevenuvnine**.

On Saturday night there was always a dinner with the Stars. During this dinner, he continued to press his case with those stars in attendance to sign his car. Unfortunately, during the dinner, he discovered that, while many of those in attendance felt flattered that a man would create such a symbol to their work, some of those at the Convention were actually laughing at him and his car behind his back and it frankly hurt his feelings. It is unfortunate that in our society, people are quick to ridicule and insult what they do not understand and many of those present simply failed to understand what Star Trek had come to mean to the world. To many of the stars, being on the Star Trek television series or in one or more of the feature films was simply an easy way to earn a paycheck by pretending to be something they weren't.

Many of those who quietly ridiculed John failed to understand what motivated this young man to even come up with the idea of a Star Trek Car. Even though he is just a normal person and will never be a member of a real Star Fleet, John was driven by a fierce desire to be a part of something bigger then himself such as Star Trek. The ridicule from some of the very people he wanted to honor hurt his feelings, and for many this would have meant the end of their dreams, but nevertheless, John Mercer persevered and continued to ask those in attendance to be part of his dream. He was elated to leave the Convention with 3 or 4 autographs gracing the exterior of his car.

While the Star Trek Convention was underway, Star Trek and his dream of creating the Star Trek Car were the most important things in the world to John, but like all things must in this world, the Convention ended and he had to return to the real world. From rubbing shoulders with the heroes of the universe, John and **Sevenuvnine** returned to the normal world, where John had to deal with the same problems as the rest of us, and the unique and unusual **Sevenuvnine** returned to being just a car.

THE Y2K BUG STRIKES SEVENUVNINE

Shortly after the Convention ended, the dangers of the Y2K bug filled the headlines. The many news stories were screaming the warning that due to these hidden computer viruses waiting to strike that the very arrival of the Millennium would result in the end of modern civilization as we knew it. There were rumors of new and even more deadly secret computer viruses spread by dooms day cults that were waiting until January 1, 2000 to strike and destroy all of the secretly infected computers throughout the world. As January 1st approached, there was a major push nationwide to ensure that all computers were Y2K compliant. So determined was the government to deal with this pending disaster than government contractors were denied new contracts if they could not prove that their computer systems were Y2K Compliant prior to December 31, 1999. John Mercer paid little attention to the hype.

However, on the morning of January 1, 2000, John Mercer left his home to drive to work[17] as he did every morning. However, on this particular day, when he tried to start **Sevenuvnine**, he discovered to his horror that his vehicle was completely disabled. He suddenly remembered all of the stories that he had heard about the dreaded computer viruses that were waiting to strike unprotected computers on this momentous day and realized to his horror that **Sevenuvnine** had a small computer in its engine. With a sick feeling, he realized that he had failed to ensure that **Sevenuvnine** was Y2K compliant. Clearly, one of those deadly computer viruses had somehow infected his beloved car. Unknown enemies had destroyed his dream while he had slept peacefully not far away.

---

[17] For sometime after creating the Star Trek Car, Sevenuvnine was actually his primary transportation.

Fortunately, the failure of the computer in his car was only a coincidence and not the result of one of the deadly Y2K bugs. After a quick trip to a repair shop and the replacement of the car's computer **Sevenuvnine** was once more ready to fly into the universe alongside of the U.S.S. Enterprise. What he had feared was the deadly Y2K Bug was actually a mechanical malfunction that was easily repaired.

THE STAR TREK CONVENTION OF 2000

In June of 2000, the Tulsa, Oklahoma Star Trek Convention was the main thing on John's mind. Determined to continue his efforts to achieve his dream of having the first recognized Star Trek Car, John Mercer called John Harper of StarBase 21 and asked if he could again bring the car out to the event in Tulsa. This time, he had changed a few things about **Sevenuvnine** to add a new dimension and a new fascination to the car. Since the last convention, John Mercer had spent a lot of time and effort in improving his car. This year, the interior of the car, which had been so torn and run down at the lat convention, was more presentable and he could have the windows down so that people could look inside. At the first event, he had covered the windows so that no one could look inside.

At this Convention, Kevin Sorbo[18], who portrayed Captain Dylan Hunt in the Science fiction series **Gene Roddenberry's**

Figure 11: Kevin Sorbo as Captain Dylan Hunt of Andromeda

---

[18] Kevin Sorbo is best known as Hercules, a legendary hero that he portrayed in the series **Hercules: The Legendary Journeys** from 1995 to 2000.

Andromeda[19] as well as **Star Trek: Voyager** star Robert Picardo[20] and other stars were making appearances and John Mercer went with high hopes of adding a number of new autographs of these well known stars. He was successful at obtaining another 6 or 7 autographs immediately and then over the length of the event, he added a number of others, though as discussed later, not that of Kevin Sorbo.

After his success at this second convention, John made the decision to get every Star Trek star on the planet to sign **Sevenuvnine**. To put his plan into operation, John Mercer started by contacting Dave Scott of Slanted Fedora Entertainment[21], the promoter of Star Trek Conventions in Las Vegas and at other locations around the country. John called Dave Scott and other promoters around the country and offered to bring his car as an exhibit for the fans to view. Unfortunately, the world was not yet ready for **Sevenuvnine** and some of the promoters refused to even consider his request, while he met with a lot of sarcastic rebuffs from others that hurt his feelings.

Figure 12: The Holographic Doctor.

BEHIND THE SCENES

As a Star Trek fan there are a lot of things that take place at a successful Star Trek convention that we do not see, such as all of the tremendous behind the scene preparation. No matter how well organized a convention may be, it is still a major challenge for the Promoter to make sure that everyone is where they are supposed to be when they are supposed to be there. A completely enjoyable convention for the fans can be a

---

[19] **Gene Roddenberry's Andromeda** was based upon ideas from the archives of the late Star Trek creator and developed for television by Robert Hewitt Wolfe. Andromeda debuted in the fall of 2000 as the number one action hour in first run syndication.

[20] Robert Picardo portrayed the Holographic Doctor on **Star Trek: Voyager** first activated during the premiere episode entitled "**Caretaker**".

[21] *Slanted Fedora Entertainment*, located at 4623 Aminda, Shawnee, Kansas. (913) 441-9405 or fax (913) 441-9406 has been promoting Star Trek Conventions for a good many years. The good people at Slanted Fedora can be contact at http://www.sfedora.com.

coordination and administrative nightmare for the promoter and his or her staff.

John Mercer discovered after two years of involvement with John Harper and StarBase 21, that even his limited participation in the preparation for a major Star Trek Convention called for him getting involved in many things that actually took a lot of the fun out of it, not to mention the approximately $5000 that it cost him each time to set up **Sevenuvnine** for the world to see.

Some time after the 2000 Star Trek Convention in Tulsa, Oklahoma, John moved to Fayetteville, Arkansas and opened his own business. He was elated to find that shortly after his arrival in this new city that there was to be a Star Trek Convention in Fayetteville. Immediately, John called the promoter of this new convention and asked to show his car. The promoter seemed somewhat puzzled by the idea of a Star Trek car, but he agreed to let John set up his display and show his car outside the facility where the Convention would be held. This was very satisfactory with John since every person attending the event would have to pass **Sevenuvnine** in order to enter the building where the Convention was taking place. He couldn't have asked for a better location.

Robert Picardo, the holographic physician from **Star Trek: Voyager** and Chase Masterson, a very lovely young lady who is best known for her role on **Star Trek: Deep Space Nine** as Leeta, a Bajoran who was married to Quark's brother. John had hoped to get Robert Picard to sign **Sevenuvnine** at the Tulsa Convention, but for some reason, it had not come to pass. So this time, he was determined that he would not leave the event in Fayetteville without a Robert Picardo autograph on the hood of **Sevenuvnine**. In preparation for this, he had added a picture of Picardo to the hood of his car and one of actress Chase Masterson to the roof. To make things even better, after a number of requests, the event Promoter had agreed to ask the stars in attendance if they would be willing to sign the car.

John was in his element, meeting and greeting those who attended and happily showing fans the one and only Star Trek car and posing for photographs. He was on such an emotional high that, when Robert Picardo pulled up in a limousine, John did not hesitate to approach this star that had become one of his favorite actors. When Picardo exited his limo the first thing he saw was **Sevenuvnine**, he naturally walked up to John and asked him what this was all about. John's response was that this was the one and only Star Trek Car and that he wanted Robert Picardo to sign it.

To his surprise, rather than being met with suspicion and caution as had happened to him in Tulsa, Robert Picardo warmly responded that he would love to sign the car and that there was no doubt in his mind that John really loved Star Trek. So it was that with a large number of fans watching closely, Robert Picardo carefully signed his name across his picture that was located on the hood of the car.

Even after signing the hood, to John's surprise, Picardo continued to examine the car in some detail and ask a number of detailed questions. He even got inside the car and discovered that there were two speakers mounted in the back seat. One speaker had Jeri Lynn Ryan's picture on it and the other speaker had another picture of Robert Picardo on it. To John's surprise, though he had not asked him to do so, Picardo leaned over and signed this second photo that was mounted on the speaker however he did not tell anyone what he signed. He continued to examine the interior before exiting and shaking hands with John.

After Robert Picardo had left to enter the convention, John leaned into the car and read the inscription that Robert Picardo had signed on the speaker. John was surprised and delighted when he read *"Making it in the back seat with Jeri Lynn Ryan,"* signed *Robert Picardo.*

Figure 13: Chase Masterson

A few minutes after Robert Picardo had finished his inspection of the one and only Star Trek Car and entered the convention, the lovely Chase Masterson[22] arrived in her own limo. John described her as being every bit as gracious as she is lovely. Fresh from his success with Robert Picardo, and with his self-confidence at an all time high, when Chase Masterson stopped to look at the car, John introduced himself and asked her if she would be willing to autograph her photo mounted on the roof of **Sevenuvnine**.

To his delight, without hesitation, Chase responded that she would be delighted to sign **Sevenuvnine**. She was wearing a very nice dress that was somewhat revealing and definitely

---

[22] Chase Masterson has sometimes been credited as Christie Carafano.

sexy, but even so, she climbed up on top of the car so that she could sign her photo that was mounted on the rooftop. As cameras flashed and fans cheered, this lovely young starlet signed the name "Chase" as large as she could across the roof of the car. For John Mercer, these two stars, by the simple gesture of signing their names, had given him a gift that money could not purchase. They had shown acceptance of the Star Trek Car!

BACK TO TULSA

Shortly after the convention in Fayetteville, Arkansas, John returned to Tulsa, Oklahoma for another Star Trek related event where he met an actor by the name of Vaughn Armstrong and some other Star Trek stars. John had become used to expressions of disbelief from the various stars he had approached for autographs, so he was very surprised in the reaction of Vaughn Armstrong. The somewhat shy dreamer and the actor, who little is anything in common, established an almost immediate rapport.

Figure 14: Vaughn Armstrong- Admiral Forester

John found Vaughn Armstrong to be one of the most down to earth individuals he had ever met. During the various events that he had attended, John had gained a great deal of self confidence so when he had the opportunity to talk to Vaughn Armstrong, John introduced himself and explained that he wanted Vaughn to sign his car. Though he had expected, and become used to, responses ranging from disbelief to amusement, to his surprise, Vaughn Armstrong seemed fascinated by the very concept of a Star Trek car.

After hearing John's request, Vaughn expressed genuine interest in why, when and how John had come to create the first Star Trek Car. The two continued their discussion at every opportunity through the event.

In his discussion of the various stars he had met over the years, John has left no doubt as to the high level of respect he has developed for Vaughn Armstrong, who had played Admiral Forest on **Star Trek: Enterprise** and is one of the few stars to have played characters on almost all of the Star Trek series[23]. He particularly mentioned how impressed he had been that, though he was a recognized star, Vaughn had treated him with the utmost respect, as he does all of his fans.

John was actually floored that when Vaughan had visited John and some friends at the hotel during the convention, that he had greeted John by name and treated him like a friend. John did not expect a star like Vaughn Armstrong to even remember his name, but instead, this star who was a part of the most important event in the world to John Mercer treated him like a friend and an equal. From such simple acts are reputations made.

I am going to end this chapter with a question that a reporter once asked John Mercer: *What does Star Trek mean to you?*

John Mercer may not have a number of advanced educational degrees and he is not the most erudite individual in the world, but he is very much aware of what that concept that is Star Trek represents for him. To this simple question, John responds with a somewhat complex answer. To John Mercer, the kid who came from a somewhat dysfunctional home, the concept that became Star Trek represents a future for mankind that shows a firm confidence in a positive future as a race and reinforcement for the idea that as a race we can literally be anything we want to be.

In the world of Star Trek you don't have to be wealthy or famous or from the "right" family; rather you can be just be a normal guy working for minimum wage sitting in some town like Fayetteville, Arkansas, but if you have enough drive and desire anything is possible. You future is exactly what you make of it; nothing more and certainly nothing less. It is a matter of desire and dedication and paying your dues.

The concept of paying your dues is illustrated by the ridicule that he still endures even after four or five conventions. He is still laughed at and teased by folks who can't seem to understand why he is doing it. Even after several years, John is still told that the concept of a Star Trek Car is the most ridiculous thing that the person making the remark has ever seen. Many people seem to think that **Sevenuvnine** is being raffled or is a part of the charity auction that takes place at each Convention. Not everyone has an appreciation for John Mercer's dream.

---

[23] Vaughn Armstrong has played more parts than anyone else on the various Star Trek series. In fact, the only Star Trek related television series that I can find that he did not play on was the original series.

CHAPTER FIVE

UNEXPECTED ROADS

Figure 15: Sevenuvnine and John - new adventures.

The first few years were rough for John Mercer and **Sevenuvnine**. Just as he had not been thrilled about his idols, Captain Kirk and Mr. Spock being replaced by a new crew on Star Trek, so it was that fans were slow to warm to the idea that there could be a Star Trek Car. After all, nowhere in any of the shows had there been anything approaching an automobile, other than one or two episodes that had been set in the past. In spite of this lack of appreciation on the part of the fans, John kept pursuing his dream.

However, things began to change for Sevenuvnine in 2002 and 2003. John's drive and obvious dedication to the concept that was Star Trek really began to pay off in 2003 as people begin to recognize and look forward to seeing the one and only Star Trek Car. Like Gene Roddenberry, John's dream became infectious and it grabbed the imagination of the Star Trek fans.

In 2002, the next convention that John attended was in Fayetteville, Arkansas. This convention had begun no different than all of the rest. As had been his custom each time he heard about an upcoming convention, John had called the local promoter and asked if he could bring Sevenuvnine and display the Star Trek Car. Unlike the disbelief he had received from promoters in the past, this time, this particular promoter was sincere when said that he would be happy to have John place his car on display.

In fact, not only was he given permission to display his car, but John had gained so much acceptance in the tight knit world of Star Trek fans that he was asked to be a part of the convention and work as a volunteer. To the small boy that lurks just beneath the surface in all of us, this was like being asked if he wanted to ride shotgun for Santa Claus. John Mercer quickly accepted the invitation; he was happy and excited to actually be a part of the convention.

Now, as a volunteer, John had the chance to see that successful conventions were not the result luck, but rather of hard work and split second coordination. In the case of the Fayetteville, Arkansas convention there was only a small budget for paying the stars to make an appearance and the promoter stressed to the volunteers that they needed to be very careful in deciding which stars to invite.

John showed up at the volunteer meeting full of enthusiasm and when he was asked who he thought they should ask to attend, John recommended Vaughn Armstrong. John and Vaughn Armstrong had kept in touch after their first meeting and Vaughn had said he would be happy to attend the smaller conventions and he promised that he not kill them financially to come to the convention. John Mercer described Vaughn Armstrong as being the most down to earth person he had ever met and one of the most flexible in regard to his financial demands to appear at a convention.

Asking Vaughn if he wanted to be a part of this particular Convention show would certainly show if Vaughn Armstrong was serious or not in his statements about not killing the promoters financially. This particular Fayetteville Star Trek Convention was not expected to draw more than 200 to 300 guests so money was extremely tight. The committee finally decided to invite Max Grodenchik[24] from *Deep Space Nine*, Robert O'Reilly[25] and Vaughn Armstrong.

The day of the show, it was raining steadily and since Sevenuvnine was sitting just outside the entrance, it was rained on throughout the show. Due to the steady downpour, no one was able to really enjoy looking at the car and few stars wanted to stand in the rain in order to autograph a car. Not even John Mercer was present to get the autographs he so greatly prized as he was slated to pick up the stars at the airport. Even so, he was able to get the stars to the show on time and everyone enjoyed the show. To John, however, he was forced to neglect **Sevenuvnine** in order to make sure that everyone else enjoyed the show. To him, it was well worth it.

The unfortunate thing to John Mercer about being a volunteer was that he didn't really get a chance to enjoy the convention himself due to the demands made on his time by his duties as a volunteer. However, he was excited about the opportunities he had to interact with the stars away from the convention. He was assigned the duties of making sure that Max was comfortable and arrived on time for each event in which he was to participate. Finally, he thought, he was well on the way to achieving his dream, little did he know that his involvement in Star Trek was to have an even more drastic impact on his life than he had ever anticipated.

NEW WORLDS TO EXPLORE

Some times when we get the chance to realize a dream, we tend to forget about the realities of the world around us. So it was with John Mercer and his dream of creating the Star Trek Car. In order to spend as much time at Star Trek Conventions as he had been doing, John had naturally had to take time off from work. Unfortunately, not everyone was

---

[24] Max Grodenchik played the character of ROM on *Star Trek: Deep Space Nine* (1993) and an alien ensign in the feature film *Star Trek: Insurrection* (1998) and furnished additional voices in *Star Trek: Starfleet Command III* (2002).

[25] Robert O'Reilly was born in New York, New York in 1950. According to his film credits, he was the voice of a Klingon *in Star Trek: The Next Generation: Interactive VCR Board Game (1995)* and the voice of Gowron in the interactive adventure entitled *Star Trek: Klingon (1996)* and the voice of Krindo in *Star Trek: Elite Force II (2003)*.

as enthusiastic about Star Trek as John. Not surprisingly, several of John's employers had given him the choice between his job and his dream. More than once he had chosen the dream over the job.

It was at this point, on the verge of achieving his dream, but unemployed once more than John made a fateful decision. The only way that he could be sure of having the time to go to the Star Trek Conventions would be to be his own box. With John, the dream was to act, so he opened his own business that he called *Computer Solutions of Fayetteville*[26].

His decision to open his own business was a decided gamble since he had little in the way of assets. This new business was a true throwing of the dice, upon which he was gambling his family's livelihood. He knew that if he could make his new dream of having his own business be successful then he would have the best of both worlds. Many times, we can be very close to achieving a dream and have everything fall apart, however, though it came as a surprise to many, Computer Solutions of Fayetteville has become as successful as John could have hoped. He was now free to achieve his other dream, the one that overshadowed all other aspects of his life, the acceptance of the first Star Trek Car.

STARS ARE HUMAN TOO

Though many seem not to know it, even movie and television stars need to have fun. None of the stars that had attended that Fayetteville, Arkansas Star Trek Convention had ever been too Fayetteville before and John decided to try and show them a good time. After the convention closed that first evening, he asked the promoters if he could borrow the limo in which he had picked up Vaughn Armstrong so that he could show them the sights of Fayetteville.

Not being really certain what stars wanted to do in the evening, he asked them where they wanted to go. To his surprise, Vaughn Armstrong replied that he wanted to swing dance and the others said that swing dancing sounded like fun. So John took them to a place in Fayetteville called Bobby Sox and they spent the evening swing dancing. That night John learned a very important lesson, that even well known television and movie stars are human too. Sometimes they just want to have fun.

---

[26] Computer Solutions of Fayetteville is located at 70 North College, Fayetteville, Arkansas 72701- (479) 444-1408- and it is located next to the Washington County Jail and across College Avenue from the Fayetteville Municipal Parking Deck.

The 2002 Fayetteville, Arkansas Star Trek Convention was smaller than most of the other conventions, but it was, in John's opinion, a very successful convention. The stars enjoyed it; the fans enjoyed it and the vendors made some money. However, the promoters did not do as well as they had hoped and, for budgetary reasons, this was the last convention held in Fayetteville.

Figure 17: Robert O'Rielly as Gowron

Figure 16: Max Grodenchik

Figure 18: John Mercer with Dominic Keeton

Figure 19: The preferred transportation of 3 out of 4 Klingons.

CHAPTER SIX

BE CAREFUL WHAT YOU WISH FOR . . .

With acceptance usually comes more responsibility and possibilities. So it was with John Mercer and the now famous Sevenuvnine Star Trek Car. This acceptance came in the year 2003 when things began to change for **Sevenuvnine**. As an example of this change, John Harper[27] invited him to come to the Star Trek Convention in Tulsa, OK.

The opportunity to display the Star Trek Car at the Tulsa Oklahoma Star Trek Convention was truly the high point of John's life. From a child of ten years old who had dreamed of meeting his idols from Star Trek, here he was at 39 years old, a part of a major convention where William Shatner, Captain James T. Kirk and Leonard Nimoy, Mr. Spock were going to be in attendance. He was going to have a chance to meet all of his boyhood heroes.

John was naturally excited at the chance to meet the original crew of the U.S.S. Enterprise. However, as happens to many of us when we are on the verge of a momentous event, John became extremely excited. The promoter, John Harper, had arranged for William Shatner to have his first photo opportunity in front of the Star Trek Car. When William Shatner came out from behind the curtain for this event, John literally pounced on him, immediately asking him to sign the car. In his excitement, the

---

[27] Owner of StarBase 21 and a truly nice guy.

amenities had been forgotten; the small boy had surfaced all at once and with a vengeance.

For the first time since he had been asking people to sign his car, he was rejected, because William Shatner absolutely refused to sign the car. In fact, as soon as the photo shoot was over, Captain Kirk disappeared back behind the curtain so fast, you would thought that Scotty had beamed him up. John Mercer was crushed.

John, being a truly empathetic individual, believes that William

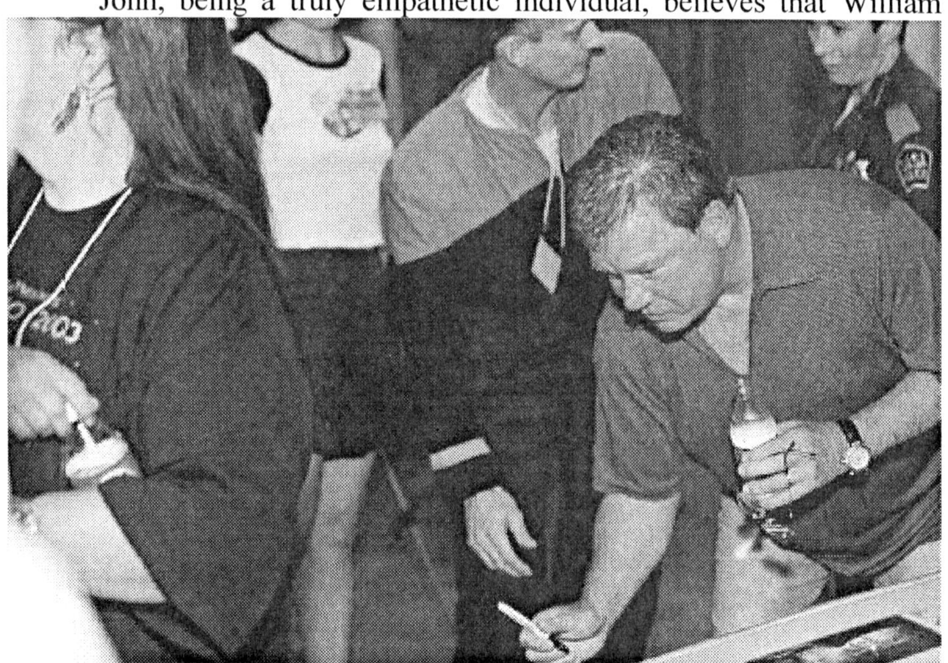

Figure 20: William Shatner signs Sevenuvnine

Shatner originally rejected his request simply because of John's overly enthusiastic approach. In hindsight, John believes that his overly enthusiastic approach made simply made Shatner feel very uncomfortable and Captain Kirk wanted to get away from the lunatic with the odd car.

In discussing this incident for this book, John made the observation that if you meet a star you have long been wanting to meet, you must stay cool and not get overly anxious. Certainly make it clear that you are glad to see them, but be careful not to make them feel uncomfortable. Otherwise, they tend to discount anything you might request and want to get away from you as soon as possible.

After a reasonable length of time had passed, John approached the police officer accompanying William Shatner[28] and asked if the officer would ask Mr. Shatner if he would reconsider John's request to sign **Sevenuvnine**. John was given the opportunity to talk to Shatner again and when he had the opportunity, John apologized for his initial approach and asked if he would reconsider the request to sign the car.

John described William Shatner as looking completely perplexed at the odd request. Finally, Shatner looked at John Harper and John Harper mentioned that everyone signed the Star Trek Car. With this support for the request, Shatner changed his mind and agreed to autograph his picture on the Star Trek Car.[29] John Mercer had achieved one of his dreams, he had met Captain Kirk and gotten him to autograph the one and only Star Trek Car.

Later in the day, Leonard Nimoy, better known as the half Vulcan Mr. Spock, walked over to examine John's car. He actually seemed somewhat perplexed at the sight of this car partially covered with autographs. According to John's description, Leonard Nimoy fit the part well; he is a very calm and a very intelligent man. Whether in costume or in civilian clothes, he has a certain way he carries himself that communicates to one and all that he has a mission. He walks with authority and radiates an aura of confidence

Figure 21: William Shatner

---

[28] When William Shatner is at a Star Trek Convention, he is normally accompanied by an individual assigned to handle crowd control issues. John Mercer is not the only one who becomes overly excited when given the chance to meet the world famous Captain James T. Kirk.

[29] When I met William Shatner at the Star Trek Convention in El Paso, Texas in 2003, I had my picture taken with him and asked if he would sign some of the books he had written that I could donate to various local charities. Initially Mr. Shatner refused, explaining that he did a lot of work for charities and if he routinely autographed everything he was asked to sign, the value of his signature would decrease and charities would be unable to use autographed items to raise money. I was somewhat taken back, but when my wife went to talk to him about autographing several items, he very graciously consented to do so. As John said, it is the manner of approach that seems to make the difference. Besides, I believe that my wife could probably convince the Devil to move to heaven.

with who he is and what he accomplished. Leonard Nimoy's very presence makes you feel comfortable.

Not wanting to make the mistake he had made with William

Figure 22: John Mercer with Leonard Nimoy "Mr. Spock"

Shatner by being overeager, John did not immediately approach Leonard Nimoy with his request that the actor sign the car, but waited for the actor to speak first. Nimoy walked to the car and, leaned forward to intently study each picture adorning the car. Finally, Nimoy/Spock straightened, looked at John and, with a very serious look on his face, and the famous raised eyebrow, made a very short comment. "Intriguing!"

Mr. Spock had spoken and this one word epitaph by the Executive Officer of the USS Enterprise meant more to John Mercer than an award presented be the President of the United States would have meant.

The reaction of William Shatner clearly in his mind, with his heart in his mouth, John stepped up to his boyhood hero and asked if he would consider autographing the Spock photo mounted on **Sevenuvnine** immediately beside the picture of Captain James T. Kirk. With an infectious smile, Leonard Nimoy looked at it John and responded with an emphatic "Absolutely!"

As John watched his hero sign the photo of Mr. Spock, he was in seventh heaven. He now had the autographs of both of his boyhood heroes. To John Mercer, with the acquisition of these two autographs,

Sevenuvnine was accepted as the one and only Star Trek Car. Anything was possible! He had now achieved what everyone had said was could not be done, like Captain Kirk in so many of the episodes of Star Trek, he had overcome impossible odds and won. No one could stop him now!

BEAM ME UP SCOTTY

To John Mercer the 2003 Star Trek Convention was an event never to be forgotten. His boyhood heroes were in the same room in which he was standing. Those action heroes that the 10 year old John Mercer had explored the universe with were now standing before him in flesh and blood. He had even shaken hands with Captain James T. Kirk and Mr. Spock and both had signed Sevenuvnine. Could there be anything better, he wondered?

His answer came a short time later when James Doohan, better

Figure 23: James Doohan aka Chief Engineer Scott "Scotty"

known as Chief Engineer Scott ("Scotty") came from behind the curtains and sat down at a table. Though William Shatner and Leonard Nimoy were the leads in the world of Star Trek, you did not have to be a Star Trek fan to know who Scotty was. Even someone who has never seen a single episode of Star Trek will recognize the phrase "Beam Me up, Scotty!"

Taking a deep breath and forcing himself to appear to be calm, John walked up to James Doohan and asked him if he would consider signing Sevenuvnine. As an aside in writing this book, John brought up an interesting point. When he first approached James Doohan, he called him Scotty, the name of his character. After the fact, he wondered if it was proper to call them by their character's name or should they be addressed by their real names. In any event, James Doohan was very gracious and responded to the well known "Scotty" as if were actually his name.

It has been interesting to note that in many cases, it is not the star who doesn't want to sign the car, it is their managers who feel that it is not something their the star would want to do. In this particular instance, James Doohan's manager, Steve, spoke up and noted that James Doohan was not in good health and had trouble getting around and, due to the size of the building in which the convention was being held, the car was about 100 yards from where James was sitting. Steve did not feel that James Doohan should be asked to walk that great a distance to sign the car.

Very much in keeping with the personality of character that he has played for so many years, ignoring this remark by his well meaning manager, James Doohan gave his well known "Scotty" smile and responded a very firm, "Absolutely, I would be pleased to sign the Star Trek Car!"

Pushing himself to his feet with some difficulty, James Doohan slowly made his way the hundred yards to where **Sevenuvnine** sat gleaming in the bright lights, awaiting the signature of the man who shall always be known as the "Chief Engineer." To John Mercer, this was one of the most awesome autographs he had ever gotten. The fact that James Doohan insisted on walking unaided from where he had been sitting to the Star Trek Car and visibly enjoyed signing his picture meant a lot. Though his body is weakening, the spirit of "Scotty" burns as bright as it ever did at his prime, when he was the main support for Captain James T. Kirk and Mr. Spock. It should also be remembered that as long as there are Star Trek fans that love and remember the shows, the spirit of "Scotty" will live on long after he has gone to explore distant galaxies in spirit.

The adventures of the original U.S.S. Enterprise were over 40 years ago and no matter how powerful a personality may be, advancing age eventually gets us all. The first to go explore what lies after this life was Deforest Kelly, Dr. McCoy and now Scotty's health is failing and his body is showing his years, but nothing can quench that charming personality except death and even then, it is not ended, just changed.

CHAPTER SEVEN

THE ADVENTURE CONTINUES

Figure 24: Sevenuvnine with the new wheel covers.

To John getting the autographs of Captain Kirk, Mr. Spock and "Scotty" were the culmination of years of dreaming. He felt that it couldn't get much better than this, however, the 2003 Tulsa Star Convention was far from over. There were more stars to meet and more autographs to get on the gleaming surface of Sevenuvnine.

The next two stars who game within phaser range[30] were two individuals whose names have long been linked by their duties on board the U.S.S. Enterprise and who are almost as well known and beloved as

---

[30] Figuratively speaking, of course.

Captain Kirk and Mr. Spock, Ensign Pavel Chekov and Lieutenant Hikaru Sulu.

For those individuals who spent the 1960s living under a rock, Ensign Pavel Chekov was an integral member of the bridge crew on board the U.S.S. Enterprise on the original missions and Lieutenant Hikaru Sulu was originally assigned to the U.S.S. Enterprise as the staff physicist, but quickly decided that he wanted to move into a more exciting position. Eventually, he became the helmsman and also assumed the additional duties of the Tactical/Weapons Officer of the US.S. Enterprise.

The popularity of both of these stars has stayed high throughout the years. There has been talk of spin off series staring both of these fine actors, though these continual discussions have not, as of yet born fruit.

Figure 25:Walter Koenig, Ensign Chekov, with Sevenuvnine.

On this momentous day, it was Walter Koenig, Chekov, who was the first one to walk up to examine the car. Fresh from his victories of having Captain Kirk, Mr. Spock and Chief Engineer "Scotty" sign the car, John was pumped up and excited. However, remembering what had happened with William Shatner when they had first met, John controlled himself as he approached Walter Koenig for his autograph.

John Mercer described Walter Koenig as being a quiet considerate man who generally kept to himself, rather than the boisterous Russian Star Fleet officer, Pavel Checkov. As he came to know the quiet star, he found that he was a very warm, gracious man who would do almost anything that a fan asked of him if it was not too unreasonable. John also found that Walter Keonig's unique accent added an unusual dimension to their conversations, as if the accent almost demanded more attention that is normally found in conversations.

When he was asked if he would sign the Star Trek Car, Walter Koenig smiled his almost shy smile and not only signed the gleaming car, but he personalized the autograph to John. It is a cherished memento to John of his meeting with a man that clearly appreciated his fans, was proud of his work and who treated everyone with respect.

The next star to come within range on this never to be forgotten Saturday was George Takei, also known to fans as Lieutenant Sulu. When George came over, John calmly[31] asked him if he would consider autographing **Sevenuvnine**. With the quiet dignity that has always marked his actions, George Takei responded that he would be honored and wrote some very interesting things by way of personalizing his autograph. He wrote a full paragraph praising John and his creation of the one and only Star Trek Car, calling it the Interstellar Shuttlecraft. It has long been John's

Figure 26: George Takei, Lieutenant Sulu, autographing Sevenuvnine.

position that he really doesn't care what a star writes on the car, as long as he or she signs

---

[31] Or as calmly as a man who was totally pumped up with excitement could appear.

it. With George Takei, he found a friend and a vocal supporter of **Sevenuvnine**.

IMPEDIMENTS TO THE STARS

The next star that John wanted to approach was Avery Brooks, the fine actor who portrayed Captain Benjamin Sisko, the Commander of the space station Deep Space Nine on the Star Trek spin off, *Star Trek: Deep Space Nine*. John never really got to know this outstanding actor beyond a casual acquaintance. John had found that most of the stars wanted to meet their fans, though many have demonstrated a desire not to be physically touched by the many adoring fans who come to see them. Most

Figure 27: Avery Brooks aka Captain Benjamin Sisko

travel with their managers and other aides who's job it is to ensure that the crowd is controlled and does not invade the actor's personal space. Unfortunately, sometimes, these aides can become overly officious and believe that they know what the stars will and will not do. When this happens, some of the joy out of seeing your hero in the flesh can be overcome with the, sometimes, rude treatment that the "keepers" dish out to fans whom they judge are too enthusiastic[32].

John had asked Avery Brooks' manager if the star would please autograph **Sevenuvnine** and was told no. Everyone he tried to talk to about asking Avery Brooks directly turned him away, stating that they were positive that Avery Brooks was much too important to autograph a car and besides they were concerned about the security aspects of him

---

[32] In defense of the Keepers, there have been many cases where fans are so into television shows or movies that they are unable to distinguish the fantasy world form the real world and actors have been injured or killed by fans. However, this protective cocoon should be tempered by the understanding that it is those adoring fans who have made the actors very wealthy people and the fans are entitled to respect.

being out in the crowd since **Sevenuvnine** was some distance away from the autograph table.

In fact there were so many people clustered around the autograph table trying to protect Avery Brooks from overly persistent fans that John was getting nowhere. He was also prohibited from talking directly to the star.

Finally, John decided that, as Captain Kirk would say, some direct action was called for, so John and some friends pushed **Sevenuvnine** from its assigned location, the 100 or so yards to where Avery Brooks was signing autographs[33]. They pushed the car up in front of the autograph table just as Avery Brooks was rising from his chair to go to the next function. John was of the opinion that only the star could give him a definite no to the request, so he repeated his request directly to the star.

Naturally, Avery Brooks was taken back by a group pushing a car up in front of him and asking for an autograph on the car, however, after understanding that John was serious, he very graciously signed **Sevenuvnine**. In fact, he seemed quite taken with the face that a fan had placed his photo on a car. There is no question that at an event such as this, the Manager wants to protect his star, the aides want to show how well they can keep people away from the star and the promoters are sometimes afraid to annoy the stars with odd requests from fans. However, if the fans do not come to these events, the actors do not make any money, so the managers and the bodyguards can't get paid and the promoter loses his shirt. It should be remembered that it is the story that captivated the fans, not the particular individuals who played the parts (except in a few rare instances). This just goes to prove that if

Figure 28: Amanda Tapping

---

[33] It was forbidden to start the engine of any vehicle inside the arena where the convention was being held.

asked, most of the stars will honor reasonable requests and it is for the star to determine what is reasonable, not his body guard nor his manager.

Amanda Tapping, also known as Major Samantha "Sam" Carter, Ph.D., from the television series Stargate SG-1 was the next star to cross John's path. When he saw her approaching, John told himself that there was no way that this beautiful woman was going to get away without signing **Sevenuvnine**. In the series, Stargate SG-1 is a gung-ho all business scientist who covers her femininity with military uniforms and carries more equipment than an army surplus store. However, John Mercer described the real Amanda Tapping as being a truly beautiful young lady to whom her uniforms on Stargate SG-1 do not come close to doing justice. She is a very outgoing person who is completely comfortable around her fans.

Though, as do all of the stars at these conventions, she walked around the convention accompanied by people assigned to protect her, she was still a completely natural person who clearly enjoyed talking to her fans. A lot of the stars do not like being touched or for anyone to get too close to them, but after signing **Sevenuvnine**, John was caught by complete surprise when Amanda through her arms around his neck and gave him a big hug. On the front fender, which is dedicated to the stars of the series Stargate SG-1, Amanda signed her picture with "Wow, this is amazing! Amanda Tapping." One and all agreed that Amanda Tapping is every bit as classy as she is beautiful.

Walking toward John, close behind Amanda, as if he was watching over her as he does in his role of General George S. Hammond in the series Stargate SG-1, came the veteran actor, Don S. Davis. Don Davis and John Mercer[34] were scheduled to do a photo shoot and at its completion, John was schedule to escort Don Davis to the autograph table as the program of activities set up by the promoter specifically stated that there were to be no autographs signed by the stars except at the autograph tables.[35] John works hard to make sure that he adheres to the programs laid out by the promoters as it makes thing run smooth.

---

[34] Each year, John Harper of Starbase 21, the promoter of the Tulsa Star Trek Convention asks John to be in charge of the photo shoots for the various stars.

[35] This rule is established in order to ensure that there is some control in the activities that take place during the convention and some of the stars also prefer to sign autographs at the autograph tables..

Figure 29: Don S. Davis, aka General George S. Hammond

However, when Don Davis had finished the photo shoot, some young fans approached the two of them and asked if Don Davis would please take the time to sign their autograph books. John told them that they would have to wait until Don Davis had gotten over to the autograph tables, but Davis interrupted and said that these were his fans and that they had come to see him. As far as he was concerned if his fans they wanted him to sign his autograph for them right now then that was the way it was going to be.

Though he plays a bluff, direct Air Force General on the series Stargate SG-1, off camera, Don Davis is the epitome of a gentleman in his dealings with everyone with whom he comes in contact and he is very appreciative and respectful of his fans.

FROM THE DEAD ZONE TO THE STAR TREK CONVENTION

Figure 30: Anthony Michael Hall signing Sevenuvnine.

The Star Trek Convention is a place to meet stars who have appeared on many different television series and movies, not just those related to Star Trek and its innumerable spin offs. John was elated to get the opportunity to meet Anthony Michael Hall, the star of television's Dead Zone.

Many will remember Anthony Michael Hall as the skinny kid with the cracked voice, painfully thin frame and wildly unkempt hair. He made a career out of playing nerds and dweebs in such films as *Sixteen Candles*[36] and *The Breakfast Club*[37] with members of Hollywood's Brat Pack. Unfortunately, his career hit a snag

---

[36] 1984
[37] 1985

as the result of some really strange behavior displayed on a personal appearance tour in 1985, but luckily for his many fans, he returned to television on Saturday Night Live later that year. In 1990 he played in the movie *Edward Scissorhands*.

Now a well spoken, strongly built young man, Anthony Michael Hall has distinguished himself as a writer and director as well as the star of the hit television series, *The Dead Zone*. Though he has absolutely nothing to do with Star Trek, he has proven to be a fan favorite at the conventions due to his eagerness to please his fans.

At the Tulsa Convention he had arrived somewhat late and was rushed to the autograph table. When his stint signing autographs was finished, as he stood up to leave he yelled out to the crowd to be sure and watch him on *The Dead Zone*, not knowing that he was soon going to be on stage before all of the fans at the convention not just the 200 or 300 in the vendor area.

In retrospect, Anthony Michael Hall is a very awesome star and John asked him to sign Sevenuvnine primarily because John remembered him from his series, The Dead Zone and because it was nice as a fan to be able to walk up to a star and introduce yourself and be warmly received by the star. Anthony Michael Hall had a very human quality about him that made it clear that he was truly interested in knowing something about his fans. If you have never met this promising young man and you see him at a convention, go up and talk to him. In 2004 Creations is sponsoring a convention that includes Anthony Michael Hall.

It is nice and certainly exciting to meet all of the big names, such as William Shatner, Leonard Nimoy, Patrick Stewart and Kevin Sorbo, but people like Anthony Michael Hall, Vaughn Armstrong, and the lovely Amanda Tapping are just the most warm friendly, awesome people you will ever meet and to overlook them in favor of the big names will be to do them and yourself as a fan a great disservice.

DAX NOT ALL FOLKS!

The many spin offs of the original Star Trek concept has given rise to a large number of stars. John has very warm memories of one in particular, Terry Farrell, who plays Lieutenant Jadzia Dax, the science officer on *Star Trek: Deep Space Nine*. Jadzie Dax was a Trill who had been joined to the Dax symbiot in the story line. Unfortunately, this bright, energetic young lady's character was killed at the end of Season Six and the Dax symbiot was placed into another character on the series.

Figure 31: Terry Farrell, aka DAX.

In person, John found Terry Farrell to be a warm, beautiful young lady with the somewhat unusual ability to put those with whom she met at ease almost at once. In their first contact, she walked up to study Sevenuvnine and John was standing nearby watching her, but wanting to give her space. After the incident with William Shatner, John was very careful to treat each star with kid gloves until he could determine how much involvement they wanted with their fans.

With these thoughts in his mind, imagine his surprise when this beautiful, well known television star turned to him and wanted to know all about the car and about John Mercer the man. [*If it has not become clear yet, let me, as the writer of this saga, interject that John Mercer, being a shy self effacing man, has not yet realized that in achieving his dream, he has become just as much a part of the myth and legend of Star Trek as Captain Kirk himself. John views himself as a nobody and is constantly surprised when these stars that he looks up to seem to instinctively recognize a connection that he has yet to understand himself.*]

Unlike many stars who merely give lip service to their fans, Terry Farrell asked questions that showed John that she was truly interested in what she was seeing and hearing. John was stunned and almost speechless when she wanted to know about him and what he did for a living. To be sure, Terry Farrell was not as bubbly and outgoing as Amanda Tapping, but she was a very comfortable, self assured young lady who saw no reason not to mingle with and more importantly, visit with her fans.

With this opening, John had no problem asking her if she would please sign her picture that he had already mounted on **Sevenuvnine**[38]. Without hesitation, she signed her photo and when she finished, she went

---

[38] Since John knew in advance which stars would be present at the Convention, he had already placed their photos on Sevenuvnine. He is a firm believer in always being prepared.

up to John and gave him a big hug, making him the envy of everyone in the general vicinity of this unusual event.

THE CARE AND FEEDING OF MOVIE AND TELEVISION STARS

Throughout these Conventions, John is continually learning about human nature and the care and feeding of movie and television stars. He had quickly learned that normally, the worst thing you can do when meeting a star is to go beyond the handshake stage or get too touchy/feely. Though the fan may feel a rapport with the star after watching him or her on television week after week, the star does not know the fan from Adam. Give the star room to become comfortable before going beyond the

Figure 32: John Billingsley signing Sevenuvnine.

handshake stage.

He had also learned that when meeting a star for the first time just listen, introduce yourself and then shut up. Many make the mistake of trying to hog the conversation. Let them talk to you and most will ask questions about who you are, what you do for a living and thank you for watching their show. Though it may not show, most of the stars are just as excited to be at the Convention as are the fans and somewhat overwhelmed that people want to meet them. Remember, stars are human too, some even have stage fright in front of large groups of people. Be understanding and empathetic and you may make a friend for life.

Figure 33: Terry Farrell signing Sevenuvnine.

CHAPTER EIGHT

MORE STARS THAN IN THE HEAVENS

Figure 34: Dominic Keeton in Sevenuvnine.

It may seem to some that John Mercer is jumping around too much in the telling of the saga that revolved around the birth of Sevenuvnine, however, John is quick to say that he is not an author and it is up to the actual writer to bring some semblance of order to this story and bring out the actual meaning of his tale. That may well be the case, however, there has been a conscious attempt on the part of the writer to relate this tale just as John told it, for in the telling is much that Spock would find "Interesting!"

<u>VOYAGER</u>

Another Star Trek spin off was a series entitled *Star Trek: Voyager*. One of the stars on this series was a very young man by the name of Garrett Wang who portrayed Ensign Harry Kim. Garrett Wang stands out in John's mind for several reasons that the writer believes go directly to the underlying theme of this book. Garrett Wang was a true gentleman, who seemed to immediately understand that Sevenuvnine was near and dear to John's heart.

Figure 35: Garrett Wang who Portrays Harry Kim on Star Trek: Voyager.

This young actor has learned at a very early age that no role is successful if it does not have a fan following. On screen, Garrett played a young, impressionable Ensign joining the U.S.S. Voyager for his first mission, however, off stage, he had an instinctive ability to actually bond with his fans that has enabled him to add luster to his acting. When John asked Garrett to sign **Sevenuvnine**, the actor clearly understood that this was an important request to the tall, thin self effacing man in the Star Trek uniform standing beside the gleaming car. Not only did Garret sign the car with his name and date, but he also added the postscript "This Car Rocks!" and signed his name in Japanese, a truly unique autograph.

Many of us are so in tune with the characters in our favorite series that we sometimes forget that they are just ordinary people like the rest of us. In the real world Garrett Wang is a very confident outgoing young man that enjoys talking to his fans. John Mercer had a very unique conversation with Garrett when the young star stepped outside into the fresh air for some "down time." was able to step outside with Garret and have a good conversation. There was no question in John's mind that the real Garrett Wang is the total opposite of the character he played on the series, he is most definitely not shy and conservative as was his character.

True fame comes not really from being on the silver screen, though that it the beginning, but more in how the fans perceive the man (or woman) behind the character. When the fans love the man, it goes without saying that the characters portrayed become more well known. As a prime example, though James Doohan the man has always been a private person, he was still a person who enjoyed others. This could not help but come through in how he played "Scotty". Though not the star of the series, he will long be remembered for his humanity and his caring ways by all of those who has the honor and privilege of meeting this man.

HERCULES DEFEATED BY FANS

Kevin Sorbo has become a very well known star of television and films, having played such roles as *Hercules* and Dylan Hunt, the Captain of the star ship Andromeda Ascending on the science fiction series *Andromeda*[39]. Though John Mercer watched and enjoyed the series Andromeda, he is first and foremost a Star Trek fan. However, he was not about to turn down a chance to meet Kevin and ask him to sign Sevenuvnine.

Figure 36: Kevin Sorbo who Portrays the Captain of the Andromeda Rising.

It was at the 2002 Star Trek Convention in Tulsa, Oklahoma that John met Kevin Sorbo, shook his hand and got an autographed photo of the star. During a lull in the chatter of the other fans clustered around Sorbo, John asked him if he would please take a moment and autograph his car. To John's shock and chagrin, Kevin Sorbo refused with a flat "NO."

With his feelings somewhat hurt, John returned to **Sevenuvnine**, unable to understand why Kevin Sorbo would take such a negative attitude

---

[39] Gene Roddenberry's Andromeda debuted as the #1 weekly hour in syndication and the rating stayed strong throughout its first season. Majel Roddenberry, the late Gene Roddenberry's wife developed the series based on a story that he had started several years before his death.

toward him. It was only later that he discovered that Kevin Sorbo has actually misunderstand what John wanted him to do. Kevin thought the car that John wanted him to sign was in the parking lot and the star, naturally, did not want to leave the building to sign a car. To him, the very idea of autographing a car made no sense. He had no idea that John was referring to the gleaming yellow car sitting some 20 feet from the autograph table.

When John pointed out that he was referring to the car on display, sitting some 20 feet away, Kevin Sorbo entire attitude changed and he responded that he would be happy to sign the car. However, as the old saying goes, the best laid plans of mice and men sometimes fail through no fault of our own. So it was with Kevin Sorbo's intention to autograph **Sevenuvnine**.

Kevin Sorbo has reached a point in his career that most stars never have a chance to obtain. At a Convention such as the Star Trek Convention, this young man cannot walk five feet without being swarmed by his fans (Usually female). As a result, his handlers keep him on a short lease. As soon as he was finished signing autographs, it was time for Kevin to go on stage to address the fans. There was a charity auction being held at the Convention to benefit a local charity. Kevin Sorbo was wearing jeans, but accompanied by the laughter of the thousands of fans in the audience, he walked on stage wearing a pair of boxer shorts over his jeans. Once on stage, he removed the boxers, held them up into the air and said "Let the bidding begin!"

To say that the bidding was fast and furious for Kevin Sorbo's boxer shorts would be an understatement. When the hammer fell on the final bid, the Kevin Sorbo boxer shorts went for the unbelievable sum of $800.00. When the lucky winner, an attractive female, naturally, came on stage to claim her prize, Kevin autographed the boxers and gave them to the winner with a big hug.

John was waiting patiently for Kevin Sorbo to come sign the car, but from the stage, Kevin was taken to the Green Room. However, to show that his heart was in the right place, he did stop long enough to promise John that as soon as he left the Green Room he would come sign Sevenuvnine.

BEHIND THE GREEN DOOR (SO TO SPEAK)

The Green Room is a private area for the stars to which only a few people other than the stars have access. The Green Room is the area where the actors can relax[40], have some food and visit with their families without the hustle, bustle and pressure of the fans. Kevin Sorbo has become such a big star that he is continually mobbed wherever he goes, especially by his legions of female fans. At a convention such as this, a star as well known as Kevin Sorbo can have serious difficult simply moving from one location on the convention floor to another. Like Avery Brooks, who played Captain Benjamin Sisko on *Star Trek Deep Space Nine*, wherever he makes a public appearance he is literally swamped by his fans.

Kevin Sorbo remained in the Green Room a little over 45 minutes and John Mercer, who did not have the proper pass that would have allowed him Green Room access stood guard mount[41] outside the door for the entire time. When Kevin left the Green Room, John was the first person he saw and John immediately renewed his request for Kevin to walk over and sign Sevenuvnine. Unfortunately for John, one of the promoters, not John Harper, who was accompanying Kevin Sorbo interjected that Kevin did not have time to sign the car as he had a flight to catch. Kevin Sorbo was no more than 20 feet from **Sevenuvnine**, but due to the mob of fans waiting to see him, he could not have made it to the car, autographed the car and have still be able to get to the airport in time to catch his flight[42].

So unfortunately, the 2002 Star Trek Convention in Tulsa, Oklahoma ended without Kevin Sorbo being able to autograph **Sevenuvnine**. John did have an 8 x 10 autographed photo of Kevin Sorbo that could have easily been affixed to the car and no one would have known that Kevin Sorbo had not signed the car. However, John Mercer is a purist, he would have known that Kevin Sorbo did not sign the car and to have added the autographed picture would have been for him to ignore the very reason that Sevenuvnine was created. The concept was for each photo on the car to be signed by the Star after the photo was placed on

---

[40] There is even message therapy available to help the stars deal with the unavoidable tensions that arise in a personal appearance of this type.

[41] Standing guard mount is certainly a familiar term to all of those who have served any time in the military. This term simply means that John waited (somewhat patiently) in location and did not move fro this location until Kevin Sorbo left the Green Room.

[42] Of course, it is absolutely possible that Kevin could have signed the car and still gotten to the airport if not for the interference of the promoter. Though many promoters think they are acting in the best interest of the stars, they are actually acting in their own best interest and this sometimes alienates fans. Had the promoter with Kevin Sorbo been John Harper, there would have been no question that Kevin would have been able to sign the car and still get to the airport. Unfortunately, Kevin Sorbo has not yet had an opportunity to place his autograph along side such signatures as William Shatner and Leonard Nimoy.

Sevenuvnine. John Mercer would not cheapen his dream by accepting anything less than the star signing the actual car.

LIEUTENANT SAAVIK, I PRESUME

Robin Curtis is a very lovely young lady who played the role of the Vulcan bridge Officer of the U.S.S. Enterprise, Lieutenant Saavik in the 1984 feature film *Star Trek III, The Search for Spock* and the 1986 feature film, *Star Trek IV: The Voyage Home*[43]. She made an appearance at the Tulsa, Oklahoma Star Trek Convention in 2003 and was very quickly a fan favorite. By this time, John had become such a fixture at the Conventions and John Harper had come to depend on him to handle the photo shoots that John had Green Room access this time. He was able to get to known Robin Curtis, as well as you can known anyone in two or three days and found her to be a warm, outgoing individual. After she posed for her pictures at the photo shoot, John asked her if she would please autograph **Sevenuvnine**.

---

[43] Lieutenant Saavik, the half Vulvcan- half Romulan Star Fleet officer, originally appeared in the second Star Trek movie, *Star Trek II: The Wrath of Khan,* in which she was portrayed by the lovely young actress Kirstie Alley. There has been little of Saavik's history given to the fans, having been cut from the film, *Wrath of Khan,* but she was born in an abandoned Roluman colony called Hellguard and rescued by Mr. Spock. She was later adopted by Spock's parents, Ambassador Sarek and Amanda Grayson. So she was actually Spock's half-sister.

Robin was fascinated by the car and spent some time reading each

Figure 37: Robin Curtis who Portrayed Lieutenant Saavik.

autograph on the car. Not only did she sign her own name on the car, but she also posed for a series of photos with John and **Sevenuvnine**. Robin has shown herself to be unique in another way, unlike many of the stars who try to keep their fans at a distance, she made it clear that she liked getting close to her fans, she didn't mind if you put your arm around her shoulders for a photo. This meant a lot to John, not in a sexually oriented way, but to him it showed that she accepted him as another person, an equal, which told him a lot about her and her outlook on life. Robin Curtis left John with nothing but good memories.

CHASE MATERSON RETURNS

The lovely Chase Masterson, best known for her role on **Star Trek: Deep Space Nine** as Leeta, a Bajoran who was married to Quark's brother, also made an appearance at the 2003 Star Trek Convention in Tulsa. She had been one of the first stars to sign Sevenuvnine and will always have a special place in the affections of John Mercer. The talents of this lovely woman have yet to be completely explored, even by her.

In addition to being a lovely woman and a fine actress, Chase Masterson has a fantastic singing voice and does a lot of entertaining when she is not in front of the cameras. She does a lot of singing and entertaining and especially likes to perform with Lolita Fatjo, her promoter, who is a talented performer in her own right.

Figure 38: John with Lolita Fatjo, promoter of Chase Masterson and other stars.

Chase remembered John and greeted him warmly, taking the time to see what new autographs had been added to the gleaming surface of the one and only Star Trek Car.

A YEAR TO REMEMBER

In the continuing saga of **Sevenuvnine**, the year 2003 is one that will live long and vibrantly in the memories of John Mercer and his wife, Trish. John's dream of the first Star Trek Car was well on its way to being universally accepted, though he had not yet achieved his goal of having every Star Trek related star autograph the gleaming yellow car.

This was also the year that John made one of his wife's fantasies become reality. Not to leave Trish out of the saga, she has been John main support system as he struggled to overcome the ridicule that most had initially heaped on he and his creation, **Sevenuvnine**. Like many wives of men who have achieved the impossible, she has stayed in the shadows, leaving her husband to occupy the spotlight. However, John was determined that she would also enjoy the long journey to achieve his dream.

Figure 39: Connor Trinneer who portrays Commander Charles "Trip" Tucker III

It was in this very important year in the life of **Sevenuvnine** that John arranged for Trish to get the thrill of her life. At the Convention, they also got to meet Scott Bakula (Captain Jonathan Archer of Enterprise), Dominic Keeton (Lieutenant Malcolm Reed), Anthony Montgomery (Ensign Travis Mayweather) and Connor Trinneer (Commander Charles "Trip" Tucker III) from *Star Trek: Enterprise*.

Commander Charles "Trip" Tucker III

On the series *Star Trek: Enterprise*, Commander Charles "Trip" Tucker III is the chief engineer on the Enterprise NX-01. Commander Tucker is portrayed by Connor Trinneer. John had long been aware that Connor Trinneer, who portrays Commander Charles "Trip" Tucker III on the new series is Trish's favorite actor and that she just had to meet him. As a surprise for his wife, John arranged with John Harper for Trish to get a pass to come into the Star Trek Convention just to meet Connor. To his utter surprise, Trish was afraid to go up and meet the man that she had long dreamed of meeting. She was standing no more than five feet from him but she was afraid to walk up to him.

Having learned long ago, that you achieve your dreams only by trying to live them, John took his lovely young wife by the hand and led her up to meet her hero, "Trip" and after she overcame her shyness, it was truly the high point of her day. Connor Trinneer proved to be a very friendly and outgoing young man with a true southern accent that seemed to charm the ladies. Whether it was true or not, the impression he gave everyone was that he very much enjoyed meeting his fans.

He also fully accepted the existence of a Star Trek car and was happy to add his autograph to the growing number of stars who had signed Sevenuvnine.

Lieutenant Malcolm Reed

John is always on the lookout for stars that have not yet signed **Sevenuvnine**, so when he spotted Dominic Keeton who portrays Lieutenant Malcolm Reed on *Star Trek: Enterprise* he approached him and asked if he would take a moment to autograph **Sevenuvnine**. At the time that John approached this young actor, he was just outside the green room practicing his the presentation before going on the stage in front of thousands of Star Trek fans. With this kind of pressure, Dominic Keeton could be forgiven if he had asked John to wait until later and John would certainly have understood. However, this very confident young actor stopped what he was doing and

Figure 40: Dominic Keeton who portrays Lt. Malcolm Reed

accompanied John over to where Sevenuvnine was sitting quietly and, after reading the comments other stars had left, he happy added his autograph.

John still remembers, and will long be impressed by the manners displayed by this young man. He treated John with the utmost respect and made it very clear that he greatly appreciated what John had accomplished and was happy to add his name to those who had gone before him. Even more than acquiring another autograph, John felt deeply honored by this young man's very attitude and demeanor.

A HAPPY MAN

By the end of the Star Trek Convention in Tulsa in June of 2003, John had achieved what many said would be impossible. He had acquired 85 or 86 autographs of Star Trek actors and actresses on the surface of

Sevenuvnine. But more importantly, he had achieved acceptance of his dream. There were still the occasional derisive comments but on the whole, more and more people looked for his car at the Conventions. But now he was ready for the big time.

Figure 41: John Mercer with Tim "Tuvok" Russ.

CHAPTER NINE

JOHN MERCER
AND
SEVENUVNINE
PLAY LAS VEGAS

There are recognizable milestones in any journey, no matter how short or how long the journey might be. One does not get up one morning and suddenly find that they are famous. There is a long pathway to follow and certain dues to pay. So it was with John Mercer and the one and only **Sevenuvnine**. The path had been long and hard, and some success had come his way, but now he was looking for a national forum to present his protégé. Just as every eagle must test its wings before flying to the highest peak, now John Mercer and his unique companion were ready to reach for the stars, as it were. John Mercer had decided that they wanted to play Las Vegas.

Las Vegas, Nevada, also called sin city, has seen it all. Every single star from the dimmest to the brightest has developed an urge to perform before the bright lights of this desert entertainment Mecca. Las Vegas had been the scene of the triumphant comeback of the King, Elvis Presley, and now John Mercer and **Sevenuvnine** wanted to follow in the footsteps of the King. This would be a litmus test of public acceptance, just as Elvis wanted to use Vegas as a guide to public acceptance, so too would John and **Sevenuvnine**.

SOMETHING IN COMMON WITH THE KING

Figure 42: John Mercer singing the theme song to Star Trek: Enterprise.

Not too many people know that John Mercer and Elvis have several things in common. First and foremost, both have chosen to live their lives in the South; Elvis, though born in Tupelo, Mississippi chose to live in Memphis, Tennessee and John Mercer though born in Oklahoma, has chosen to live his life in Fayetteville, Arkansas.

Both individuals worked long and hard to gain the spotlight. Elvis worked to bring his unique brand of music to the world and John Mercer has worked long and hard to bring his unique symbol of Star Trek, Sevenuvnine to the world. Both met ridicule and laughter[44] from the public as a result of their first efforts to achieve their dream. However, both began to achieve some success in their chosen pursuits.

However, as if these things in common were not enough, John Mercer and Elvis Presley are (or were in the case of Elvis) singers. In fact, John Mercer was even on Ed McMahon's hit television show Star Search[45]. John didn't get far, but he made it onto the little screen, a feat that is more than most contestants accomplished.

The theme song to Star Trek: Enterprise is the first theme song to a Star Trek show that actually has words to the theme song. When John heard that some of the stars from *Star Trek: Enterprise* were going to be at the 2003 Star Trek Convention in Tulsa, he went to John Harper of Starbase 21, the promoter of the Tulsa Show, and asked to be allowed to sing the theme song from the show from the stage.

---

[44] Elvis was laughed off of the stage of the Grand Ole Opry in Nashville, Tennessee and told not to give up his day job. But Elvis Presley had a dream. He worked day and night to achieve his dream and finally, he achieved heights of fame far beyond that of the biggest star of the Grand Ole Opry. There are many who would say that John Mercer, in his own way, equaled the achievements of the King – only time will tell.

[45] The original Star Search aired in the mid-1980s. This writer was unable to find any film of John Mercer singing on this popular show, but there were one or two written records that confirmed his appearance.

Now John Mercer and John Harper are good friends, but never having heard John Mercer sing prior to this unusual request, John Harper was naturally dubious. He was, I suspect, more concerned about his friend getting his feelings hurt than anything else, so he was a little slow in answering. Finally, after a great deal of consideration, John Harper replied that John had wanted to display the Star Trek Car and the fans loved it so if John Mercer would bring him a compact disc of him singing the song and John Harper liked it, then he would schedule John Mercer to sing the song at the Convention.

Now most people would have never gone as far as recording a CD of themselves singing the song; however, a little thing like recording a CD did not stop the man that had brought the world the first Star Trek Car. Not only did he record himself singing the theme song from Star Trek: Enterprise, but, to every one's surprise except John Mercer, John Harper loved it. So John Mercer was now able to add singer to his resume. Since that time, John Mercer has sung the Star Trek: Enterprise theme song at every convention where any Star Trek: Enterprise cast were in attendance.

RAISING THE BAR HIGHER

Figure 43: Even Astronauts are Star Trek Fans!

With the successful completion of the 2003 Tulsa, OK Star Trek Convention, John Mercer had now accomplished more than anyone had ever dreamed that he could. He had taken a mere dream and turned it into reality. In spite of constant ridicule, he created the first Star Trek Car and gotten a good portion of the Star Trek Community to accept it. He had promoters, who are notoriously slow to add attractions to these huge money making events that were not a sure thing of being highly successful to the various local convention, and he had sung the theme of *Star Trek: Enterprise* before a packed house at the 2003 Star Trek Convention in Tulsa, OK. What more could he hope to accomplish during one lifetime?

Though John Mercer appears, a first glance to be somewhat unsure of himself he is actually as confident and self-assured as any of the stars he had grown up watching on television. The acceptance that he was beginning to meet each time he displayed Sevenuvnine was bolstering his confidence. So no one should have been surprised when, after the 2003 Star Trek Convention in Tulsa, John Mercer went up to John Harper and told him that he wanted to take Sevenuvnine to Las Vegas, Nevada and display it at the largest Star Trek Convention in the country.

The shy country boy and his creation were wanting to go to the big

Figure 44: Gordon Michael Woolvet from Andromeda signs Sevenuvnine.

time and the bright lights of Sin City. He told John Harper that the last time he had tried to arrange to take Sevenuvnine to the Las Vegas Star Trek Convention, the promoter, Creation Entertainment had wanted $5,000.00 as a fee for John and Sevenuvnine to be part of the show. There was no way that John Mercer could raise that amount of money, but a little thing like no money was not going to stop John from showing the world that Sevenuvnine was as much a part of the Star Trek phenomenon. Instinctively, John knew that there was more than one way to skin a cat.

However, John Harper once again showed himself to be a good and true friend. Without hesitation, he called the people at Creation

Entertainment[46], one of the oldest firms that has been producing special event conventions for the fans of some of the most popular television series and films as well as providing quality merchandise for some of Hollywood's entertainment properties and pitched them the idea of having the one and only Star Trek Car at the event. John Mercer was elated when he was invited to take part in the show. Sevenuvnine would get the chance to drive in the footsteps of the King!

SEVENUVNINE HAS ENTERED THE BUILDING

The 2003 Las Vegas Convention took place August 1 – 3, 2003 at the Las Vegas Hilton, the home of *Star Trek: The Experience*[47]. This was the largest event that John Mercer had ever taken **Sevenuvnine** to since its creation.

Sometimes we try to reach for the big time well before we are ready for it. After he saw for himself the excitement and glamour that is the Las Vegas Star Trek Convention and *Star Trek: The Experience*, John began to have natural doubts. Who would want to see **Sevenuvnine**, the relatively unknown Star Trek Car when at this convention fans could see not only *Star Trek: The Experience* but also the following list of stars:

William Shatner	(Captain Kirk)
Leonard Nimoy	(Mr. Spock)
Michael Dorn	(Worf)
John Billingsley	(Enterprise's Doctor)
Robert Picardo	(Voyager's Holographic Doctor)
Tim Russ	(Tuvok)
Robbie Duncan McNeill	(Paris)
Xenia Seeberg	(from LEXX)
Robert Beltran	(From Voyager)

---

[46] For those readers who are not familiar with Creation Entertainment, the writer thinks that it is only fair to outline a little of the history of this fine company. Creation Entertainment was founded in 1971 and actually invented the concept of the touring fan convention. The company not only runs the conventions, but it also produces and distributed its own licensed merchandise from various television shows and movies. Creation Entertainment was recently purchased by Fandom.com.

[47] For those who have never seen it, *Star Trek: The Experience* is a truly mind blowing event. It is an interactive adventure based upon the voyages of Star Trek. Those who take part in this unique event are immersed in a futuristic world where they see, feel, touch and live the 24th century. Within this futuristic world are The History of the Future Museum, Quark's Bar & Grill and the largest Star Trek retail store in the world. It is the closest that most of us will ever get to the world of Star Trek.

Kate Mulgrew	(Captain Janeway from Voyager)
Ethan Phillips	(Neelix)
Alexander Siddig	(Dr. Bashar)
Nana Visitor	(Kira)
James Doohan	(Scotty)
Rene Auberjonois	(Odo)
Armin Shimerman	(Quark)
Roxann Dawson	(Torres)
Marina Sirtis	(Counselor Troi)
Paul Goddard	(Star from Farscape)
Carolyn Seymour	(Numerous chacters)
Celeste Yarnall	(Yeoman Martha Landon on TOS[48])
France Nuyen	(Elaan of Elaas on TOS)
Barbara Luna	(Lt. Marlena Moreau on TOS)
Paul Carr	(Lt. Lee Kelson on TOS)
Patrick Kilpatrick	(Numerous credits)
Glenn Shaddix	(Numerous credits)
Kurt & Cody Wetherhill	(The Borg Twins from Voyager)
Erin Gray	(Wilma Deering from Buck Rogers)
Tony Todd	(Numerous credits)
Nicole de Boer	(DAX on Deep Space Nine)

So against this line up of stars, John Mercer somehow thought that he and Sevenuvnine could hold their own. Even his friends thought that he had lost his mind and would come home crushed. However, to the shock of everyone except John (and probably Sevenuvnine and she's not talking) not only did **Sevenuvnine** hold her own against this galaxy of stars, but she became an immediate fan favorite.

---

[48] TOS = The Original Star Trek Series

In the days leading up to the Las Vegas Star Trek Convention,

Figure 45: Sevenuvnine in all of her glory.

John worked on **Sevenuvnine** until she gleamed like a new penny. The interior was redone once again, making the inside as dazzling as the exterior. New seat covered were added that had images from various shows. In fact, John treated this appearance as something that would only come around once, so he worked day and night getting the car ready. Every possible space related toy and gizmo that John could find was installed into the Star Trek car. It truly began to look like something out of Star Trek, perhaps it was now in actuality the interstellar shuttle that George Takei envisioned and referred to in his autograph.

For John, the days until the Las Vegas Star Trek Convention both drug and raced past. He was excited and looking forward to the event, but at the same time he was a little concerned that Sevenuvnine might not be ready. However, finally, the big day came, John and Sevenuvnine were in Las Vegas, Nevada. How would fans react to this country boy and his very unusual car?

SEVENUVNINE PASSES THE TEST

Sevenuvnine was set up outside the entrance to the event and John stood by nervously awaiting the reaction of the arriving fans. He was praying that all of the work and expense he had undertaken would not be for naught. The main thought on his mind was that surely, the fans that attended the Las Vegas Star Trek Convention would understand that **Sevenuvnine** was a symbol not only of the show that they all loved, but for the proposition that dreams could actually come true. He would hate to leave Las Vegas with the sounds of laughter and ridicule ringing in his ears.

The time had come, the doors to the 2003 Las Vegas Star Trek

Figure 46: Robin Curtis with John and Sevenuvnine.

Convention swung open and the first rush of fans approached. John waited nervously alongside **Sevenuvnine**, both anticipating and dreading the comments of these dedicated fans that had come a long way to see their favorite stars. Then the moment of truth arrived.

Nothing John Mercer could have anticipated would have come close to describing the reaction of the Star Trek fans in Las Vegas. As John later expressed it, *"You would have thought that these people had never seen a car before."* Almost everyone that passed by **Sevenuvnine** had to stop, look inside, read the autographs that covered the body of the car and have their picture taken with John and **Sevenuvnine**. This time no one laughed; in fact, no one expressed any sentiment except complete fascination at this car with its 86 star autographs that seemed to symbolize the essence of the Star Trek phenomenon.

The reactions of the fans that attended the 2003 Las Vegas Star Trek Convention thrilled John to his very core. He had been hoping

Figure 47: Herbert Jefferson, Jr. aka Lt. Boomer

for acceptance, but to his shock, to the fans that attended this event, **Sevenuvnine** was one of the stars of the Convention and John himself was treated with the respect normally reserved for one of the actual members of the cast of the shows. From the ridicule he had come to expect, the fans were now literally drooling over the splendor that was Sevenuvnine. As far as these fans were concerned, there was a new star in the heavens. Now John Mercer and Elvis had something else in common, both had been hits in Las Vegas.

Figure 48: Richard Herd performs at the Convention.

CHAPTER TEN

TAKING TIME FOR REFLECTIONS

Figure 49: Dominic Keeton signing Sevenuvnine.

At the conclusion of the 2003 Las Vegas Star Trek Convention, there was no doubt in anyone's mind that John Mercer had done the impossible, he had achieved the dream that he had first envisioned as a small boy growing up in Oklahoma. He had become as much a part of the Star Trek phenomenon as Captain Kirk, Captain Picard or Mr. Spock. So now, before he moved on to the next event, the Star Trek Convention in El Paso, Texas, it was time for him to pause and review all that had taken place.

WHY?

At almost every event, John has been asked why he

created **Sevenuvnine**. Even the fans who enjoyed the car the most seem to have trouble understanding why anyone would spend all of the money and time that he had put into this automobile simple to let people look at it? There was no question that he had spent an incredible amount of money achieving his dream.

There was the initial cost of the car, itself, repairing the engine, repainting it and fixing the upholstery, but that was the least amount of money that he spent in the creation of Sevenuvnine. The preservation of the autographs was a tremendous expense. Each time a star placed his autograph on the car, even if it was just one star, John had to have a layer of clear coat put on the car or the autograph would eventually wear off.

Figure 50: Ethan Phillips aka Neelix.

Before he had learned this lesson, he had lost one autograph. At a Star Trek Convention in Little Rock, Arkansas, he had gotten Ethan Phillips, who portrayed Neelix, ships cook and guide, on *Star Trek: Voyager*, to autograph the car. However, after the convention, John had not had the car immediately clear coated and the autograph faded away. To clear coat a car costs approximately $1,500.00 each time this is done and John had not had the money to get it done immediately. At the Star Trek Convention in Las Vegas, John had met Ethan Phillips again and asked him to resign the car. He is the only star who has had to sign the car more than once. However, the reader can imagine how much it has cost to clear coat the car enough times to preserve over 85 autographs.

John Mercer has not capitalized on the unique car in order to make large sums of money. In fact, it would probably be impossible for him o ever recoup what he has spent achieving his dream. So why would this young man, with a wife to support, spend so much money on something that does not return a profit? This is a question that John has never been able to completely answer, even in his own mind. However, as close as he can come to an answer is that this is his route to merge his dream with than of the immortal Gene Roddenberry.

The very idea that became Star Trek began as the dream of one man and has now blossomed into a franchise that has given not only entertainment but hope to millions. This is a future that can be if we, as a race, but strive to achieve it. So too, John Mercer's dream of creating the Star Trek car is to show that it is possible for the larger dream to come true if we persevere. What John did not realize, as he strove to achieve his own segment of the Star Trek dream was that in the achieving, he has gained a measure of the same immortality that has been achieved by Gene Roddenberry.

Each fan who sees **Sevenuvnine**, or has his or her picture taken with the unique car goes away with a little more understanding that dreams can come true. The hard work and determination can accomplish the unbelievable. As long as they have their memories of seeing **Sevenuvnine** at the Conventions or the photos exist, **Sevenuvnine** and John Mercer will live on long after John has died and **Sevenuvnine** has turned to a pile of rust. Isn't this a form of immortality?

<u>HOW?</u>

The next most asked question was how did you do it? This question was not how did he create the car, for it was obvious that he had simply purchased a car and had it painted. No, this question revolved around how the he get the acceptance for this unique symbol of Star Trek from the stars and the promoters. Those who have achieved prominence, in any field, are many times slow to help others achieve their own dreams. This is a kind of "I've got mine, the hell with you!" attitude that is shown by many of today's new crop of young stars. With this in mine, it is actually rather amazing that any of them would take the time to help an "outsider."

There is no question that when John Mercer first began to show **Sevenuvnine**, that there was little, if any, acceptance by the stars of the various series that comprised the Star Trek franchise at the time. Some stars flatly refused to sign the car, making it clear that they felt that signing a mere car was beneath them and other agreed to do it only if John paid them for their autograph. There is no question that many stars make the lion's share of their yearly income from charging for their autographs at the various conventions so, naturally, many of them wanted to charge John to autograph the car. However, what they did not and do not understand is that in the signing of the car, they achieve a measure of immortality and fame that will long outlive their participation in the vehicle that has brought them fame.

The older stars, those that have learned long ago both the price and the responsibility that comes with the fame that they achieved, seemed to intuitively understand what their participation in the Star Trek car would come to mean. Others, too full of themselves and their own self perceived importance to remember that it was fans like John Mercer who had given them their prominence, thought only of the money they were not making by "giving away" this autograph. However, this acceptance by the stars had to be earned by John, it was not freely given.

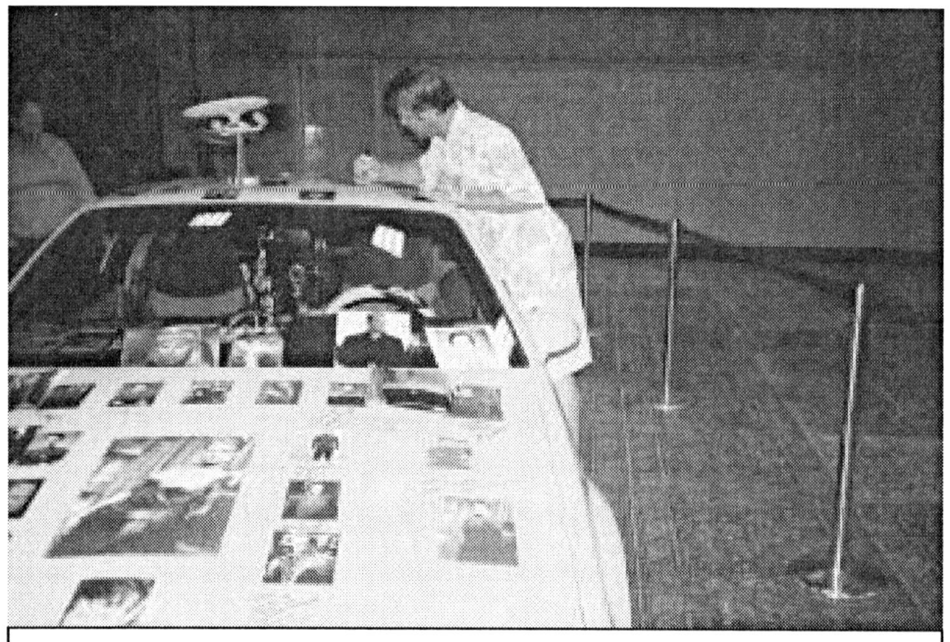

Figure 51: Another star signs Sevenuvnine.

When John first presented **Sevenuvnine**, the car was ridiculed, even by some of the stars that he had hoped to immortalize. Sadly, in the beginning of **Sevenuvnine's** career, John could not afford to pay the $10.00 or $20.00[49] that the stars wanted to charge to autograph the car, as few would go out of their way to help this quiet, shy man achieve his dream. There is no question that there have been some stars, or people who thought they were stars, whose autographs will never grace the surface of this unique car as they were too important to sign a mere car and now their 15 minutes of fame has fled and they are no longer part of the phenomenon.

---

[49] A few of the stars wanted to charge far more than this rather high sum for merely signing their names.

A Star Trek or Science Fiction Convention can be very lucrative for the stars. At some conventions, a fairly well known personality can make $12,000.00 to $15,000.00 in cash over the two or three days of the event through the selling of their autographs to the fans[50]. As of the 2003 Star Trek Convention in Tulsa, OK, John Mercer had not made a cent displaying Sevenuvnine.

Luckily for John, his business in Fayetteville, Arkansas was flourishing, but even the most lucrative small business could not hope to underwrite the cost of so many autographs and all of the other work that he has done on Sevenuvnine. In addition to the costs involved in running a business, he still has to get up each morning, pay the bills, rent, utilities, mortgage, etc. So when he was approved for the Star Trek Convention in Las Vegas, there was no way that he could afford to go that year.

LOOKING BACK

Figure 52: Tim Russ who portrayed Tuvok

Along with the autographs on the surface of **Sevenuvnine** and the fan that his participation in the various Conventions brought to him, John Mercer has acquired a lot more. He has acquired memories that he will have as long as he lives; memories that most of us would envy.

He has the memory of associating with such luminaries as William Shatner, a man not known for warm, close associations with others[51] and Leonard Nimoy, who has so much in common with his character, Mr. Spock. He has spent time with Walter Koenig and George Takei[52], and found them both to be warm, witty gentlemen.

He was privileged to meet Tim Russ, who

---

[50] Even though the writer completely understands this is an important part of the income of these stars, the very matter of fact "*give me your money and go away*" attitude of one well known personality from *Star Trek: The Next Generation* so offended the writer than he has little use for this individual.

[51] Though he does not known him well, the writer feels that it is only fair to state that in his association with William Shatner, he found him to be a gentleman of the first rank. He is cautious in dealing with those he does not know, but so too are many of us who are not in the public eye. He has achieved immortality in his life time, a feat that is accomplished by only a few each generation. Who can begrudge him his enjoyment of his fame?

[52] It was Mr. Sulu who likened Sevenuvnine to an Interstellar Shuttlecraft.

portrayed Tuvok on *Star Trek: Voyager* who signed his autograph with the phrase "Live Long and Prosper" and Ethan Phillips, Neelix on *Star Trek: Voyager*, who signed the car not once, but twice. He has had several long, in depth, conversations with Garret Wong, another rising young star who has learned at an early age, that it is the affection of the fans that make you a star, not really anything that you do or fail to do.

For John Mercer, the road has been long, but with definite high points. He can look back at having met Chase Masterson and Amanda Tapping, too beautiful young ladies who took time out from their schedules to make the dream of a shy man a reality.

He has become a part of the dream, he has met and become friends with such people as Robert Duncan McNeill who portrayed Thomas Eugene "Tom" Paris in *Star Trek: Voyager;* Cirroc Lofton[53] who portrayed Jake Sisko on *Star Trek: Deep Space Nine*; Anthony "Tony" Todd who has played a lot of Klingon roles in the various Star Trek series. Tony was also the fourth star who agreed to sign Sevenuvnine.

There was the unforgettable Alan Ruck, who portrayed Cameron Frye, a high school student[54] in the 1986 hilarious comedy *Ferris Bueller's Day Off* and Captain John Harriman in the 1994 film *Star Trek: Generations*. There was also Anthony Montgomery who portrays Ensign Travis Mayweather on Star Trek Enterprise and Alexander Siddig who portrayed Dr. Julian Bashir on *Star Trek: Deep Space Nine* who wrote *"To John, better wheels than anything we've ever come up with!"* You might

Figure 53:Robert Duncan McNeil

remember that Dr. Bashir was a real ladies man who thoroughly enjoyed DAX, portrayed by Terry Farrell.

---

[53] The writer was privileged to take part in the 2003 Star Trek Convention in El Paso, Texas and had to opportunity to meet Cirroc Lofton. Little Jake Sisko is now in college and well over six feet tall. He is one of the few child actors that the writer has met who has not let early fame go to his head. He was a clear fan favorite at the El Paso Convention and had his picture taken with a large number of young fans who were thrilled to meet him.

[54] As an interesting aside, Alan Ruck was 30 years old at the time he played the high school student in *Ferris Bueller's Day Off.*

Then there was the ever polite and gracious Michael Dorn who portrayed the Klingon Lieutenant Commander Worf on both *Star Trek: The Next Generation* as well as *Star Trek: Deep Space Nine*. Michael Dorn is one of those rare actors who truly enjoys meeting and talking with his fans. He was very happy to sign Sevenuvnine.

Then there is John Billingsley who plays Dr. Phlox on the current series, *Star Trek: Enterprise*.

He autographed Sevenuvnine with the inscription – *"To John, the first car that I have ever autographed!"*

. Many of those who have autographed Sevenuvnine have tried to stay in character. For example, Casey Biggs, who portrayed Damar on *Star Trek: Deep Space Nine* added the unique inscription *"To John, with this car I wouldn't have died in the last episode. For Cardassia!"*

He desperately wanted the autograph of Kate Mulgrew, who portrayed Captain Janeway, commander of the U.S.S. Voyager on the series *Star Trek: Voyager*. When the opportunity finally came, not only did she autograph the car, but she inscribed *"John, be gold!"*

Then there was Natalija Nogulich who portrayed Fleet Admiral Alynna Nechayev on episode #41[55] of *Star Trek: Deep Space Nine* who in addition to autographing the car, inscribed *"To John with the amazing creative vehicle."*

Figure 54:Natalija Nogulich aka Fleet Admiral Nechayev.

FROM WHERE NO ONE HAS YET RETURNED

There were also some bitter sweet memories that John carries within himself as he thinks of those who last remaining tribute, besides

---

[55] Episode is entitled *The Maquis II*.

their body of work, is their signature on the shining surface of **Sevenuvnine**. One of these who has left us is Cecily Adams, a young lady who enjoyed her fans and loved life. Cecily was the second actress to portray the character of Ishka/"Moogie" on *Star Trek: Deep Space Nine* and who enjoyed reprising this role at Star Trek Conventions for "The Ferengi Family Hour."

Cecily had taken over the role of the female Ferengi, Ishka, that was originated by Andrea Martin beginning with the episode "Ferengi Love Songs" and played the character for three more episodes. In the story line Ishka, nicknamed Moogie, was the mother of Quark and Rom.

However, fame does not insulate us from the eternal enemy of us all whether in the 21st century or the 24th century, the Grim Reaper. Though it was not evident to her many fans, the bubbly Cecily Adams had long hidden a deep dark secret, she was suffering from deadly lung cancer. Though in her own mind she had to know that her time with us was short, she did not allow this silent killer to interfere with her appearances before her fans. Unfortunately, the ravages of this deadly killer eventually overcame even her determination and love of life. In early March of 2004, this lovely lady who was only 39 years old and a fine actress died at Good Samaritan Hospital in Las Angeles, California of this deadly disease.

Cecily was the daughter of the star of the old cult television series "Get Smart" Don Adams and singer Adelaide Adams and had only recently begun to concentrate on a career as a casting director. Due in large part to her experience as an actress, she had shown great talent as a casting director. She will long be sorely missed.

As long as we are discussing those who have now gone on ahead to clear the way for the rest of us, it is only right that mention be made of a personal loss that devastated John Mercer. There are a lot of people who encouraged and supported John Mercer in his quest to create the Star Trek Car. The support of these good friends, and I include Sevenuvnine in the category of friends to this quiet man who created her, and his ability to lose himself in the world of Star Trek stood John in good stead when he had to deal with the worst personal loss that any of us can endure.

Vickie Mercer was John's mother and she had encouraged him to follow his dream from the moment that he had decided to create the one and only Star Trek Car. Frankly, she was not personally familiar with Star Trek, though she knew who Captain Kirk was from hearing John talk about him, and she did not relate to the stars as most fans do. In fact, she really didn't know what star played what character, but she was a mother.

Her son was very much a part of the Star Trek universe and she supported her son to the best of her ability.

One good thing about being the writer of a book such as this is that I can pretty much do as I please in the telling of the story. From listening to John tell the story, there is no doubt that without the encouragement of Vickie Mercer that would be no Sevenuvnine and thus no story to tell. What makes this even more interesting is that Vickie Mercer was not John's birth mother. She married his father when John was only one year old, but from everything that I have heard, no birth mother could have loved her son more.

During the 2002 Star Trek Convention in Tulsa, Oklahoma, John asked her to go with him to the dinner with the stars event. This special event is an opportunity for those who want to spend some quality time with their favorite stars to purchase a ticket to be part of the dinner and see some special performances. To Vickie, having dinner with these people that she didn't know really didn't mean that much to her, but for John to be able to take his mother to this event and for her to see the people that meant so much to her was a landmark occasion.

At the dinner, John introduced her to the actress that played the Borg Queen and to Vaughn Armstrong was had become a good friend to

Figure 55: John, Richard Herd and Vaughn Armstrong, good friends.

John. Vickie held her own, seemingly enjoying meeting these actors and actresses, but later she pulled John aside and said that he had got her to come to this dinner, but that she had no idea who these people might be. Nonetheless, she enjoyed being with her son and John was overjoyed to be able to include his mother in the world that he loved.

Fate has a way of playing ticks even on the best of us. For the night of that dinner, there was no way for John or his mother to have any idea that in a little over ninety days, Vickie Mercer would be dead from the ravages of cancer.

For those who have seen **Sevenuvnine**, the picture on the hood of **Sevenuvnine** directly below the picture of Jeri Lynn Ryan is that of Momma Vickie, the name that John had called his stepmother since the day had first met her. She might not have been his birth mother, but to John she had meant everything since she was more of a mother to him than it he had been her own flesh and blood.

ON A LIGHTER NOTE

Figure 56: Brent Strait who portrayed Rev Bem.

Returning to the less depressing memories from the earlier years, john really enjoyed meeting Brent Strait the young actor, and female fan favorite, that portrays the alien, Rev Bem, on *Gene Roddenberry's Andromeda* and who also portrayed Captain Phillips on *Roswell: The Aliens Attack.*

There was the delightful Aron Eisenberg who portrayed the Ferengi, Nog on the series *Star Trek: Deep Space Nine.* Aron wrote *"To John, Stay Strong and Sweet. Follow your dreams."* Equally as engaging was Armin Shimerman, the actor that portrayed the Ferengi, Quark on

Star Trek: Deep Space Nine. Armin inscribed *"To John, ears to you!"* This just shows that even aliens have a sense of humor.

The engaging Anthony Michael Hall is certainly one of John's favorite actors. He has an endearing quality about him, even when he is being a handful on stage. Few will forget, Wil Wheaton, the actor who first gained attention when he starred in Rob Reiner's 1986 film *Stand By Me.* Wil was still quite young when he was selected to portray Dr. Beverly Crusher's precocious son, Wesley Crusher in the television series *Star Trek: The Next Generation* and reprised the role in the 2002 film *Star Trek: Nemesis.* Wil signed the car and then inscribed *"May peace reign on earth."*

Figure 57: Aron Eisenberg, aka Nog

Robin Curtis, the lovely actress that portrayed Lieutenant Saavik has been discussed in an earlier chapter, but John still laughs when he remembers her inscription, *"John, Nice set of wheels."* Right after inscribing the car, she gave him a hug that can still light up his face.

Marina Sirtis, who played the lovely Counselor Deanna Troi on *Star Trek: The Next Generation* was the next actress to sign Sevenuvnine. As usual she was being swamped with fans, so she added no inscription, but autographed her photo that was situated right beside that of Jonathan Frakes, the actor that portrayed Captain Picard's First Officer on *Star Trek: The Next Generation.*

MEMORIES

As I sit and write this story of what happened to John Mercer in his quest to achieve his dream, I am forced to think about an incident that happened to my own cousin. As we grew up, she was a pain in the rear, but on the whole she turned out well. She married a real estate agent who was doing rather well financially and on their honeymoon, he took her to a very expensive beach resort. They had a nice dinner and then decided to walk on the beach before going to their room for some late night athletics.

Since she was dressed for a honeymoon (naturally she had to look her best), so that she could enjoy her walk on the beach in the moonlight, she took off her shoes and her panty hose. She carried the shoes and stuck her panty hose in the pocket of his suit coat where, in the excitement, they were forgotten.

Upon their return to the "real world" the suit was sent to the cleaners. When the cleaners returned the laundered suit, there was a small bag affixed to the plastic bag that covered the suit that contained the panty hose and a few "other things" that he had shoved in h is pockets and forgotten. Written on the small card that was attached to the bag by the cleaners was the one word message "Memories?"

So it is that it is the small things can remind of events that seemed so important at the time that they occurred. It is these same little thing (Not panty hose, per se) that continues to remind John of those days when he had to struggle to get recognition for his dream.

Figure 58: John Billingsley aka Dr. Phlox.

In 2001, when John only had twenty or so autographs on **Sevenuvnine**, was overjoyed to be asked to drive **Sevenuvnine** in a parade that was being held in Talico, Oklahoma. **Sevenuvnine** was being sponsored by UPN Channel 41 out of Tulsa, Oklahoma and John had high hopes that the citizens that would be lining the streets in this little town would appreciate the work and effort that had gone into Sevenuvnine.

Everyone loves a parade and even more, everyone loves being in a parade, but for none could it have been a bigger thrill than for John Mercer. As he experienced the excitement that is a parade, not matter how big or how small, he was thinking that it couldn't get much better than this. There was no way that he could know that as he proudly drove Sevenuvnine through the streets of this little town, but the biggest thrill was yet to come. When John pulled up to the speaker's platform along the parade route, he was awarded the first place trophy. Sevenuvnine had won its first award.

YOU CAN'T GET THERE FROM HERE
WITHOUT YOUR FRIENDS

Though it may appear to be jumping around to the reader, this chapter on reflections may well be the proper place to talk about some of those who have helped John achieve his dream. Though most of these people are mention in the foreword, that really does not do them justice as without them, there would not be a **Sevenuvnine**. It was John's dream, but it quickly infected those around him.

For example, John Harper is a businessman and a very good

Figure 59: Sevenuvnine, ready for the big time!

businessman. He has built Starbase 21 from a science fiction, comic book store into a major business. After the 2003 Tulsa Star Trek Convention, John Mercer went to him with his dream of taking **Sevenuvnine** to Las Vegas. As mentioned earlier, however, the problem with going to Las Vegas was not getting accepted by the promoter of the Las Vegas Star Trek Convention, Creative Entertainment, but the $5,000.00 set up fee they asked him to pay to be part of the event.

As John Mercer explained to John Harper, it was going to cost him over $2,000.00 to get **Sevenuvnine** trailered from Fayetteville to Las Vegas and $1,500.00 minimum to get the car ready. So, after these expenses were paid, John Mercer could not afford to go. Even though his business was flourishing, it didn't generate that kind of ready capital. He asked for John's advice.

It is times like this that shows someone who their true friends are. John Harper proved he was a good friend. Without hesitation, he picked up the phone, called Creative Entertainment and explained John Mercer's plight. By the time he finished talking to them, the promoter had agreed not to charge John anything to bring **Sevenuvnine**. The car would be set up as an exhibit. **Sevenuvnine** was going to the big time.

After the initial flush of excitement, reality set in with a resounding thud! John had been so determined to get **Sevenuvnine** accepted for the Las Vegas Star Trek Convention that he had not looked much beyond that. Suddenly, he had accomplished the impossible and he was accepted to bring his car to Las Vegas. He realized that in Las Vegas, 15,000 to 20,000 fans would see **Sevenuvnine**. The Convention was less than two weeks away and he needed to redo the car once more from top to bottom.

He was suddenly overwhelmed with the logistical realities. How could he get the car ready in time for the Las Vegas Star Trek Convention? Where would he get the money to pay for the upgrades? How was he going to get the car to the show? There were dozens of questions to which he did not have answers at this time. There was one thing and only thing of which he was certain -- he was taking Sevenuvnine to Las Vegas, come hell or high water.

LOOKING BACK ON LAS VEGAS

As the date of the 2003 Star Trek Convention in Las Vegas drew closer, John was getting more and more nervous. He totally and completely believed that Sevenuvnine was ready for the big time, but there were so many things that could have gone wrong. But time stands still for no man and soon it was the day to set up Sevenuvnine.

Besides showing the world Sevenuvnine, John had come to Las Vegas with an agenda. He wanted to get the autographs of Kate Mulgrew, who portrayed Captain Kathryn Janeway, Commander of the U.S.S. Voyager and Robert "Robby" Duncan who portrayed Thomas Eugene "Tom" Paris in *Star Trek: Voyager*. These two autographs placed on Sevenuvnine would complete the cast of *Star Trek: Voyager* and he was determined to accomplish this goal[56]. He had failed once before in getting Kate Mulgrew's autograph when she had to cancel out of attending the 2000 Star Trek Convention in Tulsa, Oklahoma.

Though John was still a little overwhelmed by the sheer mass of people in attendance at this convention, the volunteer staff and people in Las Vegas went out of their way to befriend this quiet young man. The volunteer staff actually helped him corral the stars and get them over to sign Sevenuvnine. In fact, John was literally blown away when he was

---

[56] Though earlier these two star autographing Sevenuvnine was mentioned, this re-telling of these events adds some more background that is an integral part of the story of Sevenuvnine.

also treated with the respect normally shown to one of the stars. He was made to feel completely welcomed and even the fans swarmed him just as they did the big stars. A large number of people, fans as well as some of the volunteer staff asked John why he did not have 8 x 10 photos of himself and Sevenuvnine available that they could purchase. He had never considered that anyone would want to purchase his autograph, but he vowed that before the next convention, he would have 8 x 10 photos of himself and his creation.

Due to fan pressure, John really did not have a chance to visit with Kate Mulgrew, though she was a lady who had long fascinated him. However, he was able to spend some time with Robert Duncan. Though he should have known better, John had made certain assumptions about Robert Duncan and what type of man he was, none of which turned out to be accurate. The star that played Thomas Eugene "Tom" Paris was totally different from what John expected. His hair was somewhat longer than it had been on the show and curly. In fact, though he had been looking for this star, John failed to recognize him initially, when Robert Duncan actually walked up to him.

When he realized who had walked up to him, John was thrilled. He found Robert "Robby" Duncan to be a somewhat laid back young man who walked up to John and started a conversation as if it was the most common thing in the world and he wasn't a star that thousands of fans had come to see. He treated John as an equal and spent some fifteen or so minutes talking to him about the car.

John had run into people at every convention who would come up and start a conversation as if they knew John Mercer. This was the first time that a star had come up to John and he hadn't recognized him. At John's request, Robert Duncan signed Sevenuvnine, and though he didn't add an inscription, it was a thrill to John all the same. With this autograph, he now had the autographs of all of the *Star Trek: Voyager* main cast members on Sevenuvnine.

The promoters had placed Sevenuvnine right beside the space assigned to Cirroc Lofton, also known as Jake Sisko, the son of Captain Benjamin Sisko from *Star Trek: Deep Space Nine*. Cirroc has long been a fan favorite and his table was a popular gathering spot for fans in Las Vegas. Since this young man was sitting nor more than three feet from where John was standing, John asked him to sign Sevenuvnine. With a flash of that devilish grin, Cirroc replied that he was happy to sign Sevenuvnine, adding the inscription *"Boldly go where no other Star Trek has gone before!"*

He again met Trish's favorite star[57], Connor Trinneer who portrays Commander Charles "Trip" Tucker III, the chief engineer on the new series *Star Trek: Enterprise*. He had signed Sevenuvnine in Tulsa, OK at the lat convention, but he stopped to spend a few minutes talking with John. He had added a postscript to his autograph that read, *"John, I can't believe that I made the hood!"*

**Figure 60: Kira Nerys
(Nana Visitor)**

In Las Vegas, John also had the chance to meet Nana Visitor, the actress that portrayed Major, later Colonel, Kira Nerys, the Bajoran second in command of the Space Station Deep Space Nine from the series *Star Trek: Deep Space Nine*. When John met her at the Las Vegas Star Trek Convention, he almost failed to recognize her. On the series, her hair is brown, but at the Convention her hair was bleached blonde. However, his initial failure to recognize this fine actress did nothing to detract from the fascination he felt for her and her acting ability. She happily signed **Sevenuvnine**, completing the list of those from *Star Trek: Deep Space Nine* that John had wanted to autograph **Sevenuvnine**.

Another star that John had been hoping to meet was Robert Beltran who portrayed Chakotay, the executive officer of the U.S.S. Voyager from the series, *Star Trek: Voyager*. This actor was brought over to meet John and Sevenuvnine by the event promoter. Once again, John found that his preconceived ideas regarding Robert Beltran were far from the mark. He is a somewhat mysterious person, similar to the character he played on the series and is typically swarmed by the fans when he makes an appearance, as a result their time to talk was limited. However, he seemed pleased by being asked to sign Sevenuvnine.

In Las Vegas, John also met another fine actor, William "Bill" Blair. Bill Blair is a highly versatile actor who has played roles in over 60 episodes of the science fiction series, *Babylon 5*; two Babylon 5 movies; over 35 episodes of *Star Trek: Deep Space Nine*; an episode of *Star Trek:*

---

[57] John is about half convinced that Trish is so taken with Charles "Trip" Tucker III because he became pregnant on the show. (Certainly something to cause a few raised eyebrows! – the writer).

Enterprise; several episodes of *Sliders*; several episodes of the science fiction series *Alien Nation* as well as numerous other films and series. Bill was happy to sign Sevenuvnine, adding the postscript "*Wheels in space, I love it!*"

Robert Lee Hawk was the sixth or seventh actor to sign in early 2000. John had watched his portrayal on the series V and had thought him a truly impressive individual. He was very friendly and out going, treating the fans with a courtesy and warmth that marked him as a true gentleman.

Richard Herd is another versatile star that John has come to know. This actor has played roles as varied as L'Kor, a Klingon on *Star Trek: The Next Generation* to Admiral Paris on *Star Trek: Voyager* to Admiral Noyce on the Science Fiction series *SeaQuest* to Supreme Commander John on the Science Fiction classic series *V*.

John had gotten to meet this distinguished actor in at the 2002 Tulsa, OK Star Trek Convention, the 2003 Star Trek Convention in Las Vegas, Nevada and the 2003 Star Trek Convention in El Paso, Texas. In fact, in El Paso, Texas, Richard Herd and John Mercer stayed in the same hotel and he managed to speak with him at some length. However, John also found that this fine actor was a man who, though certainly friendly, kept somewhat to himself. At the conventions, he was all business, wanting to meet the fans that had come to see him. Though he spent some time with John, he did not take part in any of the after hours events scheduled for the stars.

Another fond memory was the thrill of meeting Nichelle Nichols who portrayed the lovely, talented

Figure 61: Nichelle Nichols.

Lieutenant Uhura on Star Trek, the original series, at the 2002 Star Trek Convention in Tulsa. Her photograph was located on the back of the car, beside that of James Doohan, better known as "Scotty."

Both Nichelle Nichols and James Doohan have been perennial fan favorites since the beginning of the Star Trek franchise. At every convention where they make appearances, both are surrounded by groups of fans with lines waiting for autographs that stay steadily full for the 8 to 9 hours the convention ran each day. Even so, both of these truly nice people took time from their busy schedules to walk over and autograph Sevenuvnine.

Getting the autographs of these two stars from the original series was thrill enough, but both very graciously refused to accept any type of payment from John in return for their autographs. Most stars ask that John donate a sum to their favorite charity in return for their autograph, which has cost, to date for the 120 autographs now on the car somewhere around $8,000.00 to $9,000.00.

Then there was the experience of meeting Rene Auberjonois, that unforgettable actor who played Constable Odo on *Star Trek: Deep Space Nine*. John found Rene to be a true gentleman who, in spite of a list of his screen credits would fill another book, enjoyed meeting his Star Trek fans and who spoke with affection of portraying the usual character of Odo. John found him to be every bit as fascinating as the unusual character he played on the series. Very few people know it, but Rene was also originally part of the 1991 feature film, *Star Trek VI: The Undiscovered Country*. He played a character named Colonel West, but his scenes were eventually cut from the film, a definite loss to Star Trek fans.

By the time of the 2003 Las Vegas Star Trek Convention, John had gotten the autographs of the entire crew from the original series. However, the Promoter went out of his way to be helpful and brought each of these stars over to see John and Sevenuvnine. In preparation for this event, John had upholstered the passenger seat with the cast and crew of the various series. Not wanting to miss an opportunity, and certainly not wanting to offend the promoter who was trying to hard to be of help in getting stars over the see Sevenuvnine, John asked each one to also sign the seat cover. So the actors from the original series have not only signed the outside of the car, but the inside as well.

By the end of the 2003 Star Trek Convention in Las Vegas, John had the autographs of the entire original crew from *Star Trek: Voyager* except for that of Jeri Lynn Ryan, the lovely actress to the car was originally dedicated. After completing her role on Star Trek: Voyager, she took a role on the series *Boston Public* and since that series aired, she has not done a single Star Trek Convention.

However, with his drive and dedication, John has not let a little thing like her lack of appearances stop him from trying to get her autograph on Sevenuvnine. He has e-mailed everyone he can think of trying to contact this beautiful lady, but as of November 22, 2003, he has not been successful. In his mind, the car will never be complete until this actress has autographed her photo that occupies a prominent place in the center of the hood of the car. He even went to his friend John Harper, who said he didn't think that John would ever get her autograph since she does not do appearances. However, since he began his pathway to ward achieving his dream, he has always been told that this star or that star would never sign Sevenuvnine and in each and every case, he has been able to get their signatures.

He also lacks the autographs of the Captain and first officer of the Enterprise from the series *Star Trek: Enterprise*. In this current series, Captain Jonathan Archer, played by Scott Bakula is the Captain of the original U.S.S. Enterprise and Sub-Commander T-Pol, a Vulcan by birth, played by the lovely Jolene Blalock, is the Enterprises' Science Officer and First Officer.

From the series *Star Trek: The Next Generation*, he lacks the autographs of Captain Jean Luc Picard, portrayed by Patrick Stewart, Lieutenant Commander Data, portrayed by Brent Spiner and Geordi LaForge, portrayed by LeVar Burton. His goal is not out of reach; he has shown that the impossible can be achieved.

Figure 62: Don S. Davis, aka General Hammond.

CHAPTER ELEVEN

ON TO EL PASO

In spite of the thrill of taking **Sevenuvnine** to Las Vegas and the unbelievable success that he had achieved, John's 2003 had still more hurdles to be overcome. In telling the saga of **Sevenuvnine**, John cannot emphasize enough that at the 2003 Las Vegas Star Trek Convention, the fans, the few actors, or the many promoters that had fought John and the very concept of the Star Trek Car no longer seemed to exist. During the Las Vegas show, he did not hear one single remark ridiculing he or **Sevenuvnine**; he only heard praise.

In fact, he had not been ridiculed since the middle of 2003. The fans had begun to appreciate what **Sevenuvnine** stood for and were now wanting to get John's autograph, photos of himself with **Sevenuvnine** and many also wanted to have their photos taken with the unique symbol of the concept that was Star Trek. In Tulsa and especially in Las Vegas, the stars signed the car because they wanted to, not for what they would get in return. The sudden change was staggering for John. In fact, John was even approached by one individual that had appeared on the original series ask if he could please sign the car. This event was so important to John that he was literally overwhelmed, that from the original suspicion with which he had been met, he now had stars wanting to sign the car.

The car had become such a well known symbol of Star Trek and he was so close to accomplishing his original goal of getting all of the stars to sign the car, that people were now asking John what he planned to do with **Sevenuvnine**. Many people seemed to feel that he needed to offer it for sale on Ebay or some other high profile sales event. Once again, it was clear to John that people really didn't understand the underlying reason he had created Sevenuvnine in the beginning.

It was true that the car had been a major expense to John and it had not made him so much as a thin dime in return, but he had not created the car in order to make money. By his calculations as of the Las Vegas Star Trek Convention, he had put almost $45,000.00 into the car and in covering the cost of expenses in displaying the car at the various Conventions. However, achieving his dream was not about making money, but in creating a unique symbol of the Star Trek dream that lives inside all of us and in showing his dedication to that dream.

It was at the end of the Las Vegas Star Trek Convention that John realized that while he was the legal owner of Sevenuvnine, the car really belonged to the fans. People he did not know were beginning to donate toys, star ship models and such items as Klingon and Ferengi Bears to be displayed inside **Sevenuvnine.** Star were now beginning to want to autograph **Sevenuvnine** because if what it represented and more and more ordinary people were developing a visible affection for the unique car. To him, the car was achieving the same type of independent fame as the Star Ship Enterprise. How could someone sell such a symbol?

AN UNUSUAL REQUEST

Since the time that John had first created **Sevenuvnine**, he had fought almost everyone involved in the various conventions he had attended in order to be able to display **Sevenuvnine** to the fans. However, close to the end of the Las Vegas Star Trek Convention, he was totally surprised by a very attractive young lady who extended to him an invitation to bring **Sevenuvnine** to El Paso, Texas for display at the upcoming Star Trek Convention to be held in the Border town.

At first John refused the invitation because he had never heard of a Star Trek Convention being held in El Paso, Texas and, mainly, because he really did not have the money to go to another event. In fact, the $4,000.00 he had spent to get Sevenuvnine to Las Vegas had just about depleted his show funds for 2003[58]. However, the young lady that had

---

[58] In addition to the cost of hotel or motel rooms for John and his wife, there is the cost of getting the car to the event, since it is not practical to drive a car such as this to the convention as well as insurance. The reader must keep in mind that this is a one of a kind automobile and if it is involved in an accident it would be impossible to replace.

approached him, Heidi Rout from Channel 9 in El Paso, Texas is a most persistent individual. She continued to try and convince John that he had to attend this particular convention.

What many do not know is that Gene Roddenberry, the creator of Star Trek was born in El Paso, Texas. At the 2003 Star Trek Convention, the crew of the original series, William Shatner (Captain Kirk), Leonard Nimoy (Mr. Spock), George Takei (Lieutenant Sulu), Nichelle Nichols (Lieutenant Uhura) and Walter Keonig (Ensign Chekov) were going to be present and there was to be a rededication of the Gene Roddenberry Planetarium and several events to mark the location of his birth in a unique way.

Not really sure about whether or not he should try to attend the El Paso Star Trek Convention, John Mercer approached John Harper of StarBase 21. He asked John Harper had he ever heard of a Star Trek

Figure 63: Marina Sirtis signs Sevenuvnine.

Convention in El Paso, Texas. John Harper's response was that he had not heard of one and he was not planning on going to one in El Paso. Based on this information, and the fact that he really did not have the money to take **Sevenuvnine** to El Paso, John made his decision to decline the invitation.

However, sometimes, what we do not think is important can turn out to be one of the most important things in the world. The day after John

Mercer had told to John Harper about the El Paso Convention, as John was picking up the phone to call Heidi Rout and decline the invitation, John Harper called and told him that he had researched the El Paso Convention on the Internet and it looked like it was going to be a very big event. John Mercer was now torn with indecision; what should he do? He now wanted to go, but a quick review of finances made it clear that it was absolutely out of the question, he didn't have the money to go to El Paso.

<u>DON'T BE AFRAID TO ASK!</u>

Much as it pained him to do so, John Mercer made the call to Heidi Rout and sold her very simply that he just did not have the money to bring Sevenuvnine to El Paso. Very few people were aware of just how much it cost to get **Sevenuvnine** to the location where it was to be displayed. Since **Sevenuvnine** does not generate fees of any type for John, and never has, he had to front all costs out of his pocket and having just finished the Las Vegas Convention, he simply did not have the additional money available to bring the car to El Paso. Such a statement would stop most folks, but not the lovely Heidi, her response was that she wanted John and his car in El Paso and the Convention would pick up the cost of bringing the car to El Paso and the cost of his motel room as well as meals. John was stunned, this had never happened to him before. As far as Heidi was concerned, John Mercer was as much of a star as William Shatner and he was coming. She stressed to John that he was a guest, just like William Shatner or Leonardo Nimoy. No longer was he looked at as *"That guy with the strange car!"*

Still uncertain, John called Engle who had trucked **Sevenuvnine** to Las Vegas and discussed moving the car to El Paso. Engle responded that he had just purchased a covered trailer and that he would truck the car to El Paso for the cost of the fuel, an unheard of offer. With this unexpected offer, there was not doubt in John's mind that he was meant to come to EL Paso. When he mentioned to John Harper that he had been invited to come to El Paso as a guest, John Harper did some more checking into the El Paso convention and he decided to come to the convention as a participant as well. John Harper also arranged for Jonathan to bring his own unique brand of collectibles as well.

So had he not admitted that he couldn't afford to bring **Sevenuvnine** to El Paso, John Mercer would not have been offered these unique assistances and the El Paso convention would have not been as spectacular as it was.

EL PASO DEL NORTE

Figure 64: This young fan was speechless.

Having made his decision, John Mercer called Heidi as Channel 9 and said that he would come to El Paso, but that he wanted to bring Vaughn Armstrong along. Heidi assisted John in getting in touch with the promoter of the El Paso Convention[59] and without hesitation Doug

---

[59] *The Great Bird of the Galaxy Star Trek Convention* held in El Paso, Texas was organized by Heidi Rout of Channel 9 and the promoter was Planet Earth Productions, the website for this outstanding company is http://www.planetxpo.com. The floor manager for the show was a man by the name of David Welch who went out of his way to make everyone feel a part of the event. It could not have been successful without his hard work. Doug Conway is the President of Planet Earth Productions and a man who attention to detail was simply astounding.

Conway, the President of Planet Earth Productions and the promoter of the event, agreed that Vaughn Armstrong should come to the Convention.

When John had called Vaughn with the idea of the star coming to El Paso, Vaughn did not hesitate, but immediately agreed provided his plane ticket[60], hotel and meals were covered by the Promoter. This was a major concession on Vaughn's part as normally he, like most stars, receives a financial consideration to even attend an event. However, due to his friendship with John Mercer he agreed to attend in order to lend his name and perhaps help John. Vaughn Armstrong is one of the most down to earth people John Mercer had ever met and since the Tulsa show they had been fast friends. So it was that even with the purchase of the plane ticket for Vaughn Armstrong, John Mercer spent less than $1,000.00, about one fourth of what it cost him to display **Sevenuvnine** at the Las Vegas Star Trek Convention.

AN EL PASO WELCOME

John had grown up to become a man who is very self-effacing and somewhat shy. Though he is very outgoing when it comes to **Sevenuvnine**, John Mercer, the man is a very private individual. He still sees himself as the little boy who grew up watching the adventures of his heroes, so it is a shock when he is afforded to same type of treatment that is received by the stars. John was treated by everyone with whom he came in contact as if he were a well known star. He still marvels that he was made to feel as he were one of the most important people on the planet.

From the time he arrived in El Paso, everyone he met was excited about getting a chance to see the car. Due to the nature of **Sevenuvnine**, John is naturally careful about letting is be exposed to the elements. However he was assured by everyone that it had not rained in El Paso in three months, so there was nothing to worry about on that account. However, with the usual unpredictability of El Paso weather, less than an hour after car was rolled off of the transport trailer it began to rain. The car has been clear coated several times, but he still does not like it exposed to the elements if he can help it.

---

[60] John Mercer has never told Vaughn that he personally paid for the plane ticket to get Vaughn to El Paso. The promoters paid for the hotel and the meals for the star.

Figure 65: Heidi Rout and Friend, John Collins.

Heidi had planned to feature **Sevenuvnine** in a lot of the advertising leading up to the event, so she had asked if he and Vaughn Armstrong would come to the Channel 9 studios to do a live interview on the News at noon. John was finding it a little hard to understand the complete change between the previous ridicule and the current attitude supporting **Sevenuvnine**. However, not being slow on the uptake, he knew he had to take advantage of the positive attitude pervading this event.

Heidi Rout had wanted John and Vaughn Armstrong to come to the Channel 9 Studio for a live interview on the News at Noon. So John, with Vaughn behind the wheel of **Sevenuvnine** drove from the hotel to the Channel 9 Studio in downtown El Paso for the interview. The mere appearance of this very distinctive car on the streets of El Paso quickly drew a crowd. Additionally, **Sevenuvnine** has tremendous performance speed and power, so Vaughn Armstrong, who is used to the high-speed freeways of California, was in his elements as they cruised down Interstate 10. The rain made the streets somewhat treacherous, but Vaughn's experience and Sevenuvnine's power overcame this minor annoyance. Only a few people other than John Mercer have ever driven Sevenuvnine, such as Robert Picardo, Chase Masterson, and Casey Biggs. Now Vaughn Armstrong's name could be added to this select group.

Shortly before the noon hour on this particular Friday before the beginning of the Convention on Saturday, Vaughn and John pulled into the parking lot of Channel 9. The crowd that was waiting for them were simply awe struck by Sevenuvnine and were very enthusiastic in their welcome. The entire time, John was thinking that if these people only knew what he had to go through to get to this point, they would be amazed. John was finally beginning to feel that he was close to realizing his dream.

LIKE FATHER, LIKE SON

There was one person waiting in that crowd for John that gave him a real thrill, Gene Roddenberry, Jr., the son of the legendary creator of Star Trek. John had gotten Majal Roddenberry[61], the lovely wife of the late Gene Roddenberry and Rod's mother, to sign **Sevenuvnine** at an earlier event, but he had never had the pleasure of meeting the son, known by all as Rod, before this interview. Rod Roddenberry is probably one of the nicest young men in Hollywood and he stepped forward to meet John as he left the car. He and John Mercer quickly became friends.

As mentioned above, Rod Roddenberry had not yet signed **Sevenuvnine**, so he decided to show his support for John and **Sevenuvnine**. With the cameras, Gene Roddenberry, Jr. introduced **Sevenuvnine** as one man's dream and the symbol of one man's dedication to Star Trek and the legend of his father[62]. Then in front of the television audience, Gene Roddenberry, Jr. autographed **Sevenuvnine**.

When John was interviewed, he was asked what he planned on doing with the car once he had achieved his goal of every star signing it. John's reply was that the car was not a commodity to be sold, but rather a symbol of his dedication to the concept that is Star Trek and he could not sell it because it actually belonged to the fans. The fans had made the car what is had become, he was just the man who was the current caretaker of this symbol of the future.

No matter where John went while in El Paso, people wanted to know what John planned to ultimately do with the car. The concern shown by the fans for this automobile approached that level that would be sown for a much beloved uncle or some other person that the asker was fond of. This type of concern for a mere car was far beyond what John had actually

---

[61] Majal Roddenberry originally played the first officer on the original pilot, Nurse Chapel on the original series of Star Trek and Counselor Troi's mother on *Star Trek: The Next Generation*.

[62] Prior to the cameras rolling, John Mercer cautioned Rod that the name of the car was **Sevenuvnine**, not Seven of nine as he did not want to run afoul of the trademark and copyright laws since Paramount owns the trademark Seven Of Nine. With an infectious grin, Gene responded to let him worry about paramount. This writer can only make the observation that this young man is a chip off the old block.

expected. The answer to this question was hard for John because he is not really sure what he plans to do with **Sevenuvnine**. He would prefer placing it in a Star Trek museum should Paramount or Gene Roddenberry, Jr. ultimately decide to create one.

To be sure, he would like to get some compensation for his hard work and dedication to recoup some of what he has invested, but at no time would this entail selling his beloved **Sevenuvnine**.

THERE'S ONE IN EVERY CROWD

John Mercer and Vaughn Armstrong drove away from Channel 9 with the cheers of the fans ringing in their ears. The plans called for John to take his car to the Convention Center on set it up inside the Center where the event would take place. There had been no problems up to this point and once **Sevenuvnine** was in place, the work was done until it was time to load the car for the return trip home. So with high spirits the two pulled up to the entrance ramp at the rear of the Convention Center and John asked the guard how to get **Sevenuvnine** inside the building. That was when the problems started.

In every organization there is someone who is overly officious who wants to throw his weight around and make it clear that he is important. In the Convention Center Staff, this individual was the Fire Marshal. John was told in no uncertain terms that he could not display **Sevenuvnine** inside the building on the specific orders of the Fire Marshall[63]. Without bothering to inspect the car, the Fire Marshall had decided that allowing the car inside the Convention Center would be a fire hazard, Nothing that John or Vaughn could say about the safety features of the car[64] had any impact on the Security Guard at the Convention Center and the Fire Marshall did not put in an appearance. The edict had been issued; this car was not going to enter that building.

Needless to say, to John, this was highly upsetting as he had come a long way and a lot of money was being spent so that he could display

---

[63] Names have either not been used or changed to protect the officious.

[64] Sevenuvnine has a shut off which disconnects the fuel and starter so it cannot be started inside the building. There was no danger of some child getting inside the car and trying to drive it away or the exhaust fumes making people ill or starting fires. Unfortunately, as is many times the case when dealing with petty officials who's egos get involved in their jobs, the Fire Marshall did not know this and did not want to be bothered with facts.

Sevenuvnine for the fans. Sitting the car out front of the Convention site was not really an option due to the continuing possibility of inclement weather and the searing heat that could also damage **Sevenuvnine's** finish. However, nothing he said swayed the Security Guard.

When all else failed, John Mercer called Heidi Rout and told her the problem. A Texas Tornado has nothing on the force that this little lady can bring to bear on someone that gets in her way. This young lady left her job at Channel 9 and came to the Convention Center to deal with this issue and the unreasonable attitude of one man who was determined to put a damper on the enjoyment of the many fans who would be filling the Convention Center the next day. It only took Heidi a few minutes to straighten out this little problem, but throughout the Convention, a few of the Security guards and other employees of the Convention Center caused periodic problems for vendors and Convention organizers alike.

A FAMILY EVENT

Another aspect of the Star Trek phenomenon that has caught John Mercer's attention is that even today, the show has caught the attention of many of the young. Most children in our modern society have their own interests that more often than not exclude the adults. So when something catches the imagination of a child that is also of interest to the adults, it brings the parents and the children closer together. This was true when John was captivated by the original series and it is true today.

Also many of the young are car fanciers, as were their fathers before them. So Sevenuvnine is also common ground for both the young as well as the parents when it is displayed at a Convention. Having come from a very dysfunctional home, his mother was married 14 times, he can state from a first hand perspective that anything that can act as common ground for the child and the parents is a very important part of the experience of growing up.

SETTING UP IS HARD TO DO

Returning to the adventures of John Mercer and his car at the El Paso Convention, Heidi Rout had overcome the objections of the Fire Marshall and cleared the path for John Mercer to drive **Sevenuvnine** into the Convention Center. However, even though he was now inside the building, no one had any idea where he should park the car so that it would be shown in the best light for the fans.

John Harper of StarBase 21 was already set up close to the front of the vendor area and was somewhat unhappy that John had been late arriving. He had saved John an area for the car near his booth that had now been taken by another vendor. John Harper had not been aware that Channel 9 wanted to do an interview with John and Vaughn Armstrong, so he had finally allowed someone else to take the spot he had reserved for **Sevenuvnine**. Now that **Sevenuvnine** was a fan favorite, vendors vied with each other to have the car set near their booth space, as it was a fan magnet. Unfortunately, there was no longer any available space in the front of the Convention Center space that was allotted to the vendors where John could set up his car.

The relationship that John has developed with the various vendors

Figure 66: Sevenuvnine is a fan magnet.

at the conventions where he displays **Sevenuvnine** is somewhat unique. The vendors take part in the events to offer products to fans that can not be found locally, whether it is an action figure, or a toy or some other item from one of the science fiction series, such as Star Trek, or SG-1 and it is important for someone who has a non-profit generating display such as **Sevenuvnine** to have a good relationship with vendors. John has formed long lasting friendships with many of the vendors and over 90% of the vendors with whom he has come in contact have contributed to the charity auctions at the events or directly to support **Sevenuvnine**. If there is something that he needs for the car, the vendors organize and find it, many times donating the item, at no cost to John. In return, John endeavors to draw the most fans possible to the car that results in more sales by those vendors located immediately around the car's location.

Figure 67: Find Sevenuvnine and you will find the stars!

It is also interesting to note that since the Tulsa Star Trek Convention in 2003, the stars also tend to gravitate toward **Sevenuvnine**. At every Star Trek Convention there is always a photo shoot featuring the stars in attendance that involves **Sevenuvnine** in some fashion. If a fan is interested in getting close to a particular star that is attending a Star Trek Convention, simply stay close to the car and the star will come to them.

This change in attitude toward Sevenuvnine did not come overnight, but as a direct result of hard work, dedication, and a great deal of expense on the part of John Mercer. Though no one had said anything about this to John, there is certainly a realization on the part of the vendors that John is always there and incurring expenses in supporting the dream of Star Trek and making no effort to make anything off of his dream. So it says a great deal that these vendors, who are there only to make money, happily donate much of what John needs of make **Sevenuvnine** better, such as a picture of a star of a doll or a Star Trek related toy. **Sevenuvnine** has become a recognized part of the Star Trek Universe and the Vendors look at it with great affection.

John also has something else in common with the Star Trek vendors, and that is the hard work involved in setting up **Sevenuvnine** for the fans to view. Once the location is determined, the car is parked and the shutoffs engaged to ensure that the car cannot be restarted until after the event has concluded. Then the car is given a coat of Armor All from front to rear and the wax finish touched up until it gleams. The sound system[65] and the lights as well as all of the space aged gadgets are tested to ensure that everything is in working order. Only then can John take time out for himself, just as the cowboy would see to the needs of his horse before taking care of himself, so too does John Mercer care for **Sevenuvnine** before looking to his own welfare.

Figure 68: Even the Borg try to recruit Sevenuvnine.

---

[65] On this setup day, there was no music playing any place in the Convention Center so John played Star Trek related music though the Sevenuvnine sound system throughout the afternoon which made the work seem lighter to those vendors sweating to set up their displays. This is something else that is always greatly appreciated by the many vendors with whom John has come into contact.

Figure 69: Great Bird of the Galaxy by Michael David Ward

CHAPTER TWELVE

THE GREAT BIRD OF THE GALAXY
STAR TREK CONVENTION

Finally, the big day, Saturday Nov. 15, 2003 arrived. This was to be the first day of the Great Bird of the Galaxy Star Trek Convention in El Paso, Texas. This was the largest show of this type to be attempted along the border, and fans lined up early to see the original crew of the U.S.S. Enterprise who were all scheduled to appear at this event.

<u>THE ARRIVAL</u>

John and **Sevenuvnine** arrived in El Paso on Thursday, November 13th. He normally makes a point of arriving at each new city early to that he is not rushed in the setting up and he also enjoys taking part in the welcoming of the stars as they arrive. On this night, he drove Sevenuvnine from the Chase Suites, the motel in which most of the stars were booked, to the El Paso International Airport in order to pick up Vaughn Armstrong, who was scheduled to arrive about 8:15 PM. This began a memorial night for John.

He made the trip form the motel to the Airport in **Sevenuvnine** with all of the lights and sounds working. People stopped and stared, fascinated by this very unusual car, unlike anything normally seen in this Bordertown. It was only a few blocks from the motel to the airport, so it was a rather short ride. Engle followed behind in order to let Vaughn's luggage be loaded into his car as **Sevenuvnine** does not have a great deal of trunk space. However, once the luggage was loaded, Vaughn made it very clear that he wanted to ride in **Sevenuvnine**, so he and John left the airport with all flags flying, lights flashing and sounds blaring. El Paso never knew what hit it!

Heidi Rout had invited John and Vaughn to go out to dinner, but Vaughn was too tired so John called her and asked for rain check. However, less than thirty minutes later, Vaughn called John and said he wanted to get something to eat. So after a great deal of discussion, it was decided to try the small nightclub not too far from the Chase Suites called Mavericks. Since the night spot was close, it was decided to walk, so John, Vaughn and Engle walked over to Mavericks.

Once inside, the three took a table and ordered a meal and drinks. Vaughn Armstrong insisted on buying John a drink, thought John felt that he should be buying drinks for Vaughn. There was some friendly disagreement over who would buy what for whom, but finally, to keep the peace, John ordered a beer and Vaughn ordered a scotch on the rocks for himself. The atmosphere was pleasant, the food was good and drinks weren't watered, so all in all it was a great evening, but then it was decided that John and Vaughn would play some pool.

Now playing pool with Vaughn Armstrong is an interesting endeavor. John rates him as something of a pool shark, though Vaughn denies it vehemently. John was sure he was going to lose, but he knew that he would enjoy the game no matter how it came out.

While they were playing, three very attractive ladies entered the night spot and put their quarters up on the edge of the pool table in the age old signal that they wanted to play after John and Vaughn finished. One of the three kept eyeing Vaughn as if she recognized him so John announced to everyone in the room exactly who Vaughn Armstrong was and why he was in El Paso. Now John knew that Vaughn wanted to strangle him because this was just going to be an evening of relaxing, but Vaughn ever the gentleman, spent a great deal of time talking with the patrons of the club, who were all fascinated that he was a star.

The reception that both John and Vaughn received at Mavericks was typical of how they were treated throughout their time in El Paso. Everyone welcomed them to El Paso with open arms and could not seem to do enough for them. John was just blown away that they treated him with the same respect, bordering on awe with which they treated Vaughn.

Finally, after a number of requests, John returned to the motel and got photos of Sevenuvnine and Vaughn and almost everyone in the club received an autographed photo. Even the owner of Mavericks insisted on having autographed photos of each of them that were put up inside the bar for the world to see. In spite of the star treatment, both thoroughly enjoyed the evening.

THE REDEDICATION

On Friday night, there was a special invitation only event hosted by the El Paso Independent School System (EPISD). This special event was for the rededication of the Gene Roddenberry Planetarium that is located in the School District Headquarters. The various dignitaries and stars in attendance at this special event were introduced to the crowd of fans by Gene Roddenberry, Jr.. Gene Roddenberry, Jr. (called Rod by most), the son of the legendary visionary has taken over the helm of the family business and has shown himself to be a worthy successor to his father.

Figure 70:Gene Roddenberry, Jr.

At this star studded gala, the poster commemorating the event was unveiled and the artist signed copies and the fans swarmed over the stars asking for their autographs. It was an evening enjoyed by all who were privileged to attend.

A SURPRISE INVITATION

On this very special Friday night, Heidi Rout came to John and invited him to join her and the stars for dinner. Now at most events there was a dinner with the stars, and John always made a point to attend. So he told Heidi that he would be happy to join the group for dinner. It was at the dinner that John made the contacts that eventually resulted in the stars autographing Sevenuvnine.

When John arrived at the local restaurant, imagine his surprise

Figure 71: After this night Nichelle Nichols always remembered his name.

when the dinner turned out to be a very small, private affair for the stars and about twenty guests. What made this small event even more special for John was that the entire crews from the original series was present for this event[66] For the first time, he was able to spend some quality time with those individuals that had been his childhood heroes.

He has fond memories of this intimate dinner. The first person he spoke to was Nichelle Nichols, who he had originally met at the Tulsa Star Trek Convention. She said that she remembered his face, but could not place his name. After John re-introduced himself, she called him by name every time she saw him for the rest of the event. She is every inch a lady and one of the most talented performers to appear on the series. Her singing has thrilled millions of fans around the world.

For John the invitation to this dinner made the entire trip

Figure 72: How many get to have dinner with Lieutenant Sulu?

worthwhile. He was able to get several pictures of himself with each of the stars and make a number of new friends. To John this was a unique honor that had been extended to him. Of course, to Heidi Rout, it was unthinkable that he not attend the dinner for the stars, for he is now viewed by many as one of the stars himself. Heidi had invited John on the same basis upon which she invited the stars and to her that was all there was too it. This is a mental transition that John is slow to realize.

---

[66] The entire crew of the original Enterprise came to El Paso to honor Gene Roddenberry except for Deforest Kelly who was deceased, William Shatner who was scheduled to arrive on Sunday and Leonard Nimoy who was scheduled to arrive the next day, but who was eventually forced to cancel his appearance.

THE GREAT BIRD OF THE GALAXY FLIES

John arrived at the event early, about 9.30 AM, in order to make sure that Sevenuvnine was as bright and shiny as it could be for the fans that would be viewing the car. Just as he had everything as perfect as possible, the promoter came over to ask if he would mind moving **Sevenuvnine** to another location as the car was sitting just about where they planed to have the stars stand for their photo sessions with the fans.

Now on the face of it, the request to move the car was a simple one and the promoter did not seem to feel that it was causing a problem for John, but appearances can be deceiving. Once **Sevenuvnine** was parked and the final process was begun to make the car show ready, all systems were shut off. This meant that the car had absolutely no power. In fact, the lights, sound system and all of the other attachments that needed power in order to operate were not run from the car batteries, but from extension cords plugged into power outlets. **Sevenuvnine** was not able to move under its own power and if he had to power the car up to move it, it would take over an hour before he would have the car ready for the fans. The doors were scheduled to open in less than fifteen minutes.

Then the promoter asked if the car could be pushed to a new location. There was no reason that this could not be done, but John was not capable of pushing **Sevenuvnine** to a new location by himself. As a result, the promoter gathered some of the workers to help and the car was carefully pushed to a new location. Once the brakes were locked again, John quickly got the car ready for display just as the doors were opened for the fans. It was a close thing and John was comfortable with the new location.

John was standing in front of Sevenuvnine as the fans came rushing into the vendor area. The excitement had begun and it would be two days of Star Trek toys, models and stars.

CHAPTER THIRTEEN

AN EXCITING SATURDAY
IN
EL PASO DEL NORTE

When John arrived in El Paso, he really didn't need any additional autographs as he already had obtained the autographs of all of those stars present. However, the promoters went out of their way to get the stars to come over to **Sevenuvnine** and sign the car. This gave John not only a chance to renew acquaintances with many of them, but many of the vendors had given him various types of Star Trek memorabilia[67] and he had the chance to get the stars to autograph the actual items.

Sevenuvnine was sitting next to the booth of Ken Hudnall[68], who is the writer of this book, and his wife Sharon. Throughout the Convention, they shared their hospitality with John and Vaughn. This also

---

[67] This included action figures of many of the stars and other star trek related items.

[68] Just for clarification, I am not a Star Trek Vendor, per se, but Heidi Rout had offered me the opportunity to have a booth in return for the donation of copies of a book I had written on the ghosts that haunt El Paso that were placed in the gift baskets given to each star. She also invited me to bring any Star Trek or Star Wars items that I wanted to sell. I was sure that I had only a few items but when Sharon and I finished going through closets and opening boxes, we had over 4,500 items. I brought them all to the Star Trek Convention. – The writer

gave them a chance to socialize and eventually, Sharon Hudnall made the suggestion that a book be written about how the first Star Trek Car came to be created. From this suggestion, John Mercer and Ken Hudnall arrived at an agreement to create a unique book detailing this unusual saga.

A SLOW START

Since he had been to a number of Star Trek Conventions, John was concerned that the early of the Convention on Saturday was somewhat slow. John talked to Heidi and found out that the promoters had planned the main part of the show around the appearances on Sunday of Leonard Nimoy[69] and William Shatner. Heidi assured John that Sunday would produce more traffic than the Convention would be able to contain.

That is not to say that there was not a large crowd on Saturday, for the flow of fans was fairly steady throughout the day. A large number of people made purchases at the booth of Ken & Sharon Hudnall and most vendors made decent sales. The number of people who came to see **Sevenuvnine** and Vaughn Armstrong was respectable.

Figure 73: Author Ken Hudnall with Cirroc Lofton (Jake Sisko) from Star Trek: Deep Space Nine.

There were a lot of people who wanted pictures of the car and this was the first time that John had tried to offer to autographed photos of

---

[69] Unfortunately, at the last moment, Leonard Nimoy had to cancel his appearance due to pressing business concerns.

Sevenuvnine and himself in order to attempt to defray some of the cost. On this somewhat slow Saturday, he told 15-20 autographed photos, far more than he had thought he would be able to sell.

There were two stars at the Convention whose autographs John did not have on the shiny surface of **Sevenuvnine**, Tony from Star Gate SG-1 and Herbert Jefferson, Jr., who portrayed Lieutenant Boomer on BattleStar Galactica.

It was at the El Paso Convention that John decided to dedicate one half of the driver's side door to the BattleStar Galactica series. Even though this series was not one of the Star Trek franchise, it was still a program that he had enjoyed watching as a young man. He only has one star's autograph from this series as of this time, but some of the former stars of this classic series are starting to appear at conventions. Over time, he plans to get all of them that are still available. Sadly, Commander Adama, Lorne Greene has left us, but the majority of the stars are still around.

So Saturday finished without a lot of excitement. Vaughn Armstrong was introduced from the stage to a fairly large audience. Afterward, a lot of the fans present had the opportunity to talk with him and he told them of some of his adventures. John was able to spend more quality time getting to know the rest of the stars. Then sadly, the El Paso Star Trek Convention finally shut down for the night and everyone returned to Planet Earth.

THE REVELS CONTINUE

Rather than return to their motel immediately, John and Vaughn Armstrong went to the Camino Real Hotel, which was located across the street from the El Paso Convention Center. In the Restaurant of the hotel, they found a small party already underway. In attendance were Nichelle Nichols, George Takei, James Doohan, Walter Koenig and the rest of the stars in attendance at the Convention.

Nichelle greeted him by his first name, as did the rest of the stars. It made John feel very accepted, as if he had accomplished some great feat by just being able to be in the same room as these household names. This gathering lasted into the small hours of the morning before the various parties in attendance decided it would be wise to get some sleep before Sunday's show.

SUNDAY

Sunday rolled around the as Heidi had promised it was busier from the moment the doors were opened. Many more people had bought Sunday passes this was the day that William Shatner was supposed to be speaking.

The Convention Promoter came to John and said he had heard that

Figure 74: James Doohan and Ken Hudnall

John had sung the theme song from the Star Trek: Enterprise series at some earlier conventions and asked if he wanted to introduce Vaughn Armstrong and sing the song for the fans of El Paso. John was extremely flattered but he responded that he would be happy to introduce Vaughn, but that he had not come prepared to sing and he was not cleared the sing that song at this Convention. In spite of his objections, the Promoter continued to urge him to sing and finally he agreed perform the song. The crowd absolutely loved John's rendition of the song and enthusiastically applauded the appearance of Vaughn Armstrong.

After leaving the stage, Vaughn and John came back to the autograph table and this time John was the center of attention as the fans were overwhelmed with John's singing. To the fans, John was as much a star as Vaughn Armstrong or anyone else at the convention. In only a couple of hours, he signed and sold over 20 autographs, this response was absolutely blowing his mind.

For John, this was a convention of firsts; this was the first convention where he had not had to work, or pay to get the autographs of the stars and this was the first time that he had offered to sell autographed photos of himself and Sevenuvnine. This was also the first time he had been called upon to do an impromptu song for the audience that had been well received. He was on an emotional high that lasted for sometime.

**Figure 75: John performing
the theme song from
Star Trek: Enterprise.**

Along with requests for his autograph, John was asked a lot of questions about his plans for **Sevenuvnine**. For some reason, there is a large contingent of fans who expect him to sell the car for a large profit to some collector. As he has said earlier, John would like to see the car in a Star Trek Museum so that all of the fans can continue to see the unique Star Trek Car. He feels he has about two years more before he has all of the autographs he is seeking, with the biggest challenge being that of Jeri Ryan, so there is still time to find a permanent home for his beloved **Sevenuvnine**.

<u>A FEW OBSERVATIONS REGARDING THE EL PASO EXPERIENCE</u>

Before this section regarding the El Paso "Star Trek Convention is finished, John Mercer wanted to make sure that some closing remarks were added to this chapter. These remarks are actually his observations about personalities and events that took place in El Paso. In spite of his professed inability to express himself, John's insights into the personalities and events that took place in El Paso certainly are worth reading.

It has been John's experience that at each event there are one or

Figure 76: Artist Michael David Ward (r) meeting his fans.

two people who stand out either for their actions, their personalities or both. One of those that impressed him the most in El Paso was a young man by the name of Michael David Ward[70]. Michael David Ward is an artist who is expert at reverse glass painting. He has created unbelievably beautiful works of art honoring almost all of the science fiction television series such as *Star Trek*, the original series; *Star Trek: The Next Generation*; *Star Trek: Deep Space Nine*; *Star Trek: Voyager* and many others of the classic series.

John had the opportunity of meeting and talking to Michael for sometime and he was very impressed with both the young man as well as

---

[70] Michael David Ward is the master of reverse glass painting. Samples of his work can be found at his website. The website address is http://www.Lightspeedfineart.com.

his talent. After the invitation only dinner with the stars, everyone went to the Gene Roddenberry Planetarium for the rededication of this educational facility. After the stars were introduced to the fans waiting impatiently to see their heroes, everyone went into the Planetarium where a demonstration of the Planetarium program was run for everyone to see. This monument to the legendary Gene Roddenberry has given a lot of El Paso school children an appreciation for the wonders of space and a number of local personalities and some stars spoke about the man behind the idea. Then last of all, there was a display of the artwork of Michael David Ward, much of it inspired by the work of Gene Roddenberry and examples of the unbelievable talent of this young man. One of the pieces he painted was given to Buzz Aldrin, one of the astronauts that walked on the moon.

A UNIQUE HONOR

John Mercer spent a great deal of time getting to know this talented young man and recognized a kindred spirit. Michael's talent and the medium in which he works is not run of the mill and he had to work hard to achieve public acceptance just as John had to struggle to have his dream accepted by the public.

Sevenuvnine was a dream dedicated to the world of Star Trek, but John has collected the autographs of other stars who either have impressed him as a person or whose series John found impressive. John was very much impressed by the talent of Michael David Ward and even more impressed by the dedication that he recognized equaled his own. There are a lot of negative people in the world who try to block those who display unique or special skills from achieving their dreams. Michael had endured ridicule and overcome it just as had John.

With this in mind, John Mercer gave Michael David Ward the highest honor that it was within his power to bestow. He asked the young artist if he would autograph **Sevenuvnine**. On his part, Michael David Ward had already seen Sevenuvnine and knew what it meant, both as a symbol and to the man, John Mercer. So, Michael very astutely understood the honor that John was offering to him and clearly showed his surprise asking John is he was sure he wanted Michael to sign **Sevenuvnine**. If there were any lingering doubts, this question removed them, John was adamant that he wanted the young artist, a friend of the late Gene Roddenberry to sign **Sevenuvnine**.

The next day Michael came over to where Sevenuvnine was parked and John gave him a pen to use to sign the car. John gave him a space on the rear and told Michael that he could do whatever he wanted with it. After a moment, Michael signed his name, but then continued to embellish his autograph. Around his signature he placed stars and planets and among them, the original USS Enterprise. The drawing, though in black and white, looked awesome.

As he studied the drawing, John thought to himself that if the drawing had some color, it would be perfect. So he asked Michael if he would add color, if John furnished him a set of colored felt tip pens. Michael responded that he would be more than happy to add color to the drawing. That night Engle purchased a set of colored pens and when John saw Michael the next day John waved the set of pens at him and repeated his request that Michael add color to the fantastic drawing. Michael was happy to oblige and when he finished adding color to the back tailgate, John had a work of art that would cost several thousand dollars if he had purchased it.

John tried to express his unbelievable gratitude at what Michael had done, but the young man cut him off and responded that he was the one that was honored by being asked to even sign the car. Throughout their association, John Mercer found Michael David Wardto be one of the most down to earth, friendly people he had ever met.

OTHER UNFORGETTABLE PEOPLE

There were two other people in El Paso that John found to be unforgettable. One was the lovely Heidi Rout, the Channel 9 representative who worked so hard to make sure that there were no problems. This was the second Star Trek Convention in El Paso and the second one that Heidi had helped to organize. She is a unique personality, who brings a ray of sunshine into every room into which she enters.

Another person, Doug Conway, President of Planet Earth Productions[71] and the Promoter of the event, impressed John as not only being a professional and a business man, but also as being someone who cared about the vendors and exhibitors that came to the show. He and his staff tried to do everything in their power to make the event enjoyable for every participant. It is the promoter's job to get the stars to come to the

---

[71] Planet Earth Productions, LLC is located at 27499 River View Center, Bonita Springs, Florida 34134.

event, taking care of their hotels, meals, airfares and paying any fees that are required to guarantee their appearances. Doug Conway handled this with a generous good nature that removed all of the normal stress found in such an event. For someone relatively young, he was a true professional and it showed in the way he handled not only details but people.

Then, though John has talked about the lovely Heidi Rout and her efforts to make the Convention run smoothly, enough cannot be said about Heidi and her dedication to brining this Convention to the people of El Paso. Without Heidi and others who worked with her, such as John Collins, there would have been no way that the Promoter could have made this event a success.

For John, the El Paso show was a very well organized show and things ran so smoothly that there was very little stress placed any of the participants. Everyone remarked on how welcome they were made to feel when they first arrived in El Paso and the first impression is very important to the stars. At some shows, he has seen the stars be very tense and feel rushed; they clearly do not enjoy themselves and can become very vocal about their unhappiness. In El Paso, every participant felt relaxed and it showed in the interaction between the celebrities and the fans. If only all shows could be as well organized as the one in El Paso.

Figure 77: Nichelle Nichols, George Takei and Walter Koenig at the rededication of the Roddenberry Planetarium.

CHAPTER FOURTEEN

ASSORTED MEMORIES
FROM
BEHIND THE SCENES

DON'T LOOK BEHIND THE CURTAIN

When the Wizard of Oz told Dorothy not to look at the man behind the curtain, he was attempting to keep her form finding out that everything is not what it seemed. The same is true with almost anything that has become such a phenomenon as the Star Trek franchise. The fans of the series suspend their rational mind for the duration of the episode and do not stop to analyze what makes the various incidents happen.

When you are a fan of Star Trek and have the opportunity to attend a Star Trek Convention, you buy a ticket, sometimes an autograph ticket[72], sometimes only a generic ticket[73] or premium tickets, such as the prized gold ticket[74]. Once the fan has purchased the ticket of his or her choice, they are able to enter the exhibitor and vendor areas and check out all of

---

[72] This ticket allows the holder to get a certain number of star autographs with the payment of just one fee.

[73] This ticket just allows the holder entry to the event. To get autographs of the stars, or to attend special events, additional sums are required.

[74] The premium ticket allows the holder to attend certain special events, met the stars and get the autographs of all of the stars present at the Convention.

the neat souvenirs available for purchase as well as opportunities to meet the stars, as authors and other relatively famous personalities. Just the fans suspend their rational minds during the watching of the episodes of their favorite shows, so too they enter a different world populated by their heroes.

Before creating **Sevenuvnine** and becoming part of the world he had long envied, John had attended a number of Conventions and been thrilled by everything he had seen. Only after he began to attend Conventions himself as an exhibitor, was he allowed to look behind the curtain and discover the totally different world that existed out of sight of the fans.

A BIG DOSE OF REALITY

The first Convention that John Mercer attended with **Sevenuvnine** was the Tulsa, Oklahoma Star Trek Convention held in June of 1999. Never having done anything like a Convention before, John had no idea what to expect. In spite of his own fears, he actually expected to have a good time associating with the stars and other exhibitors. Unfortunately, nothing prepared John for the reception he received from the heroes of the science fiction world.

Very few understood what John was attempting to do with **Sevenuvnine** and he had to endure a lot of ridicule and snide remarks from not only the fans, but even some of the stars he was attempting to honor, and certainly the other vendors did not make his life easier. Most of these people did not know and did not care that their cruel remarks hurt this man's feelings. For the actors, some took the attitude that they were big stars and he was beneath them; to them he was someone to laugh at. They never stopped to think that this was the same treatment that the legendary Gene Roddenberry received when he first put forward the idea that became Star Trek. Has Gene Roddenberry been discouraged by the ridicule and not created the Star Trek series, then many of these actors would have spent their time pumping gas or in some other less visible occupation.

John wanted to get each star he met to sign **Sevenuvnine**; he had not stopped to consider how they would react to his requests. With the excitement of a small boy, he approached his heroes and asked them to autograph his car. Almost all of them laughed at first, but then they asked for $20.00 or $30.00 or even $50.00 to autograph the car. Sometimes the star would come up and ask John if they could autograph the car. With barely contained excitement, John would show them where to sign and then they would ask him for $20.00 or $30.00 dollars for the autograph. To the stars, John seemed to be an easy mark to purchase their autographs; to John sometimes these dollars represented food on the table for he and his wife.

There were other times when an actor he wanted to get to sign **Sevenuvnine** would be on stage in front of the fans. The Promoter would tell John that as soon as the actor left the stage, he had to run to catch his flight so John had to wait at the stage door to catch the star if he wanted the actor's autograph. Sometimes John would wait by the stage door for an hour or more with nothing to do but stand in that one spot. It seemed as if the major stars would fly in for the morning and then fly back out in the evening. They spent very little time at the Convention. In these days, John had no one to assist him or look out for his interests so he had to do everything himself. Those were cruel, heartbreaking days as he learned that his heroes were not the giving, understanding people he had watched on television.

John specifically remembers when, at his first convention, he approached a young lady who had not been a main star, but a mid-level character on a Star Trek episode entitled Apple. John asked her if she would sign the car and explained that he was not making anything from his appearance and that he would like her to donate her autograph. Her response was that this was how she made her money and that she would not give away her autograph. John asked her how much she charged and she told him that she received $20.00 per autograph. He asked her how much she wanted to autograph **Sevenuvnine** and she responded $50.00. She was adamant that she would only sign **Sevenuvnine** if she were paid to do so.

John had thought that the reason for the Star Trek Conventions was for the fans to be able to meet their favorite stars. He was not finding out that the real purpose behind the Star Trek Conventions was for the stars, the promoters, and the vendors to make money. It was somewhat disillusioning to this idealistic young man that his heroes were actually human like the rest of us. He had firmly thought that a Star Trek Convention was about buying a ticket and getting to meet William Shatner or Leonard Nimoy or Avery Brooks. Instead, it was about nothing but money for the stars.

Though in defense of this very commercial attitude on the part of some of the people who think they are bigger stars than they actually are;

in many cases living on their past glories is the only income that some of these people have. Either their series was cancelled and they cannot get another part, or they have become type cast, such as George Reeves did with the part of Superman from the 1950s television show. When it is impossible to get acting parts, this is when you see former stars acting as security guards or filling other types of relatively unskilled jobs. This is why when they have the opportunity to sell their autographed or their photos they are loath to give them away, no matter how worthy a cause.

Sometimes you get yourself in a situation where you are working for an hourly wage and you could not give the star what they want for their autographs. Since, in the beginning, John was working for an hourly wage, there were times he just simply could not afford to attend the convention, but he did anyway. He would take money from here or there just to be at the Convention knowing full well that when he got home there would be hell to pay in regard to personal finances.

John has now paid his dues, so to speak and generally he does not currently have to pay for stars to place their autographs on Sevenuvnine. With that said, he did have to pay Herbert Jefferson, Jr. for his autograph in El Paso, and he paid Richard Herd and Tony from SG-1. Just because his car is at a Star Trek Convention, he does not have the ability to say sign my car, each star is different.

A LOOK BEHIND THE CURTAIN

Though the promoters come into town with their own paid, experienced staff members, it is the local volunteers that really make a Star Trek Convention function. Most of these volunteers were originally fans who wanted the opportunity to get a chance to meet the stars and saw this as a way to do it without paying the high prices at the ticket booth. While this is one benefit of being a volunteer, in exchange it can be hard, dirty, thankless work.

YOU CAN'T GET THERE FROM HERE

When fans see **Sevenuvnine** gleaming in the lights of the auditorium or convention center or other local where the convention takes place, they are in awe at the sheer beauty of this machine. Few, however, stop to think how difficult it can be to get an automobile such as this form its home garage to the location of a Convention. In some cases it would be absolutely impossible without the assistance of one special individual, Engle.

John first met Engle at a Star Trek Convention in Tulsa, OK about three years ago. This young man first studied **Sevenuvnine** from every angle before approaching John; opening the conversation as most people do by saying that he absolutely loved the car. Then he asked John how he had gotten the car to the convention site. John responded that he had driven **Sevenuvnine** from his home to the site of the convention[75]. Then Engle made an offer that John just could not believe. He offered to trailer the car for John if John could get him a Gold Ticket to the convention with

Figure 78: Nichelle Nichols is a fan favorite where ever she goes.

Green Room Access.

Naturally, John discounted the offer since the cost of transporting a car like **Sevenuvnine** would be many times the cost of a Gold Ticket to the convention. With these thoughts in mind, John thanked him kindly and

---

[75] At this point in time, John lived in Clairmont, OK, so it was not that long a drive and Sevenuvnine was routinely used as John's primary transportation.

then dismissed it from his mind. After all, in John's experience, when something is too good to be true, it usually is.

Shortly after this convention, John and his wife moved to Fayetteville, Arkansas. They did not return to Tulsa, until the following year when they were once again at the Tulsa Star Trek Convention. Once again, Engle came over and studied the car form every angle, before approaching John and asking him how he had gotten the car to the convention site. John replied that he had driven the car from Fayetteville to Tulsa, a 4 or 5 hours drive. Engle again renewed his offer to trailer the car to the conventions in return for a Gold Ticket with Green Room

Figure 79: Dominic Keeton enjoyed his time at the Convention.

access. This time John agreed.

John had asked John Harper of StarBase 21 to help him be invited to the Las Vegas Convention. So as soon as John Harper told John that he had arranged for him to be part of the Star Trek Convention in Las Vegas, John asked Engle if he really was serious about his offer to transport Sevenuvnine to a convention. Not only was he serious, but Engle drove from his home in Norman OK to Fayetteville, Arkansas, loaded the car onto a flatbed trailer and John into the cab and drove the long empty highway to Las Vegas, Nevada. True to his word, he only asked for the Gold Pass with Green Room Access so that he could meet the stars.

John felt guilty that Engle was willing to transport **Sevenuvnine** and asked so little in return, so he helped to cover expenses. Even with John's contribution, Engle still spent a lot of money getting the car to Las Vegas, but with the promise of the Gold Ticket, Engle didn't care. Once they arrived at the Convention, John immediately coordinated with the Promoter and arranged for Engle to have full access to all areas of the show. This was a true win/win situation for everyone and Engle was in seventh heaven.

As mentioned earlier, it was at the Star Trek Convention in Las Vegas that John received the invitation to being **Sevenuvnine** to the Star Trek Convention in El Paso, Texas. John was a little hesitant to ask Engle if he would transport the car all the way to El Paso, but finally he broached the subject. To his surprise, Engle did not hesitate before responding that for a Gold Ticket and with a sixty day notice, he would happily transport **Sevenuvnine** to any convention within the Continental United States. So arrangements were made for Engle to come to Fayetteville, Arkansas in early November to pick up John and **Sevenuvnine**.

However, when Engle arrived to pick up John and Sevenuvnine for the trip to El Paso, John was stunned at what his friend had done. Not being satisfied with transporting **Sevenuvnine** on a flatbed truck, Engle had purchase a very nice enclosed trailer big enough to transport not only **Sevenuvnine**, but also all of the items that fans had donated to upgrade the fabled Star Trek car[76]. Engle's rationale for spending almost $9,000.00 for a state of the art car transport trailer simply to carry **Sevenuvnine** was that the car was still in danger of being damaged, and certainly exposed to the elements, if carried on an open flat bed trailer. If John had any doubts about Engle's dedication to the goal of **Sevenuvnine**, this gesture settled the matter once and for all. With this one gesture, Engle had earned his Gold Ticket many times over.

Even with the purchase of a first class transport for **Sevenuvnine**, there were still some technical problems to be overcome. A Camaro runs low to the ground, which means that if there is any grade at all that must

---

[76] From laughing at Sevenuvnine, fans have now gone out of their way to donate such things as Star Trek Bears, Klingon Bears and a large number of other items of every shape and type. John takes the issue of fan donations very seriously. As far as John is concerned, these items are not his, but they are part of the Sevenuvnine project. These things, as well as the car, now belongs to the fans, John Mercer is just the caretaker for the moment, for how can a man own a dream?

be climbed to enter the transport the car can ram the front bumper into the surface. Having anticipated this problem, Engle had built a special ramp to get the car onto the enclosed trailer without any danger of hanging up the front bumper.

Engle has become an integral part of the **Sevenuvnine** team, not only does he transport the car, but once it is in position at the Convention, he helps clean, polish and ensure that everything is functional and ready for fans. If there is something that must be obtained, then he is the one that runs for what is needed. His efforts are greatly appreciated, as he does not have to do any of these things. If, once the car on was the ground he disappeared to party, no one would blame him, for in return for a Gold Ticket worth only a few hundred dollars, he transports the car with a care that John himself would who, an effort that would normally cost in the neighborhood of $1,500.00 per trip. He has also contributed over $10,000.00 from his own pocket. A man like Engle is rare; he is a good friend to John, a godfather to **Sevenuvnine** and an adherent to the dream.

Figure 80: The illusive Jeri Ryan.

CHAPTER FIFTEEN

A FEW REMARKS FROM THE FIRST OFFICER OF SEVENUVNINE

<u>CHAIN OF COMMAND</u>

In the telling of the saga of **Sevenuvnine**, there is no doubt that in the minds of the many fans who now donate souvenirs and other items, some very expensive, to dress up the car, that it has achieved a status similar to that of the original Enterprise[77]. This being the case, there is no doubt that if there is a chain of command, there is no doubt that John Mercer is the Captain of the Interstellar Shuttlecraft, **Sevenuvnine**.

While serving as the Captain of any type of craft is a fantastic emotional charge, there can be no success without the support of a loyal crew. John Mercer is most fortunate to have as his first officer, the lovely Trish Mercer, his patient, long suffering wife. It was her imagination and support that led John to finally set out to achieve his childhood dream. Without Trish there could have been no **Sevenuvnine**.

This being said, it is only fair and proper that the First Officer of the Interstellar Shuttlecraft be called upon to give her observations and tell her stories of the creation of this most unusual symbol of the Star Trek

---

[77] It should also be remembered that no less a personality than Lieutenant Sulu, (George Takei) has christened **Sevenuvnine** as the first Interstellar Shuttlecraft.

franchise. She was there even before the beginning and she saw and intuitively knew things that not even John was privy to, and I am sure that she had her doubts about this crazy dream, but it was her husband's dream and she supported it.

Trish Mercer is a pretty, slim blonde whose main goal in life is to support the efforts of her husband. When John talked about the sacrifices that he made to get to this point, it goes without saying that Trish also made the same sacrifices. When he suffered the rejection of the stars and the fans, she suffered along with him, not for the rejections but for what those rejections did to John. When he wanted to stop, it was Trish whose quiet confidence at his ability to achieve his dream that kept him going.

**Figure 81: Anthony Michael Hall, Trish Mercer and
Some Guy Hovering In the Back.**

AS TRISH REMEMBERED

When John Mercer sent me the tapes for what became this book, he had one tape that was Trish recording her memories of events. Even though I, the writer, has never met John's wife, a great deal can be told from listening to her tell the tale.

First, there is no question that she is very much in love with her husband and supports his efforts completely. She has a soft voice, which leaves me to believe that she is also somewhat shy, just as John is, in his own way, somewhat shy. But what I found the most unusual is that is also came across that she also completely supports John's dream. Throughout the tape, she referred to **Sevenuvnine** as an individual. To her, thus mechanical marvel, though to most of us just a machine, has achieved the status normally attained by a child, a daughter if you will.

As Trish tells the story, after a great deal of discussion, they went looking for a car that John could use as the focal point of his dream and after a lot of looking, they finally found "her" at a used car lot. When they first saw "her" she was gray, with big wheels. There was absolutely nothing that would make this car stand out, in fact, it looked rather worn, but something caught their eye. That something could only be described as potential. Perhaps instinctively, like called to like. Perhaps **Sevenuvnine** also had a dream and to "her" John and Trish had the potential to help the car realize her dream. Neither of them were ever able to say just why this particular car was chosen, but the moment they laid eyes on this car, John knew that this was the one that he wanted. To Trish, if that was the car John wanted, then that was the car he would have.

Once John brought the car home, there was no doubt in her mind that the car needed a lot of work, but even so, there was something about the car that just called to them. John began to refer to the car as KITT[78], but for reasons she could not identify, Trish decided that this name was not suitable for this car. The car needed a more distinctive name.

As most husbands do John had his own game plan, of course, but Trish suggested to John that he take the car to a paint shop. The dark gray color just did not suit the car she pictured in her mind. She told John that she though that the car should be painted a bright yellow similar to the hair of Jeri Ryan and that he should name the car **Sevenuvnine**, after the character that Jeri Ryan portrayed.

As John recalled earlier in this saga, he did not originally do as Trish recommended and he was not satisfied with the original paint job, even though it was a very expensive paint job. Eventually, he had the car painted a bright yellow as she has suggested. As Trish related, the car was

---

[78] The original KITT car was the Knight Industries Two Thousand from the television show Knight Rider.

painted yellow[79], the windows were tinted and a nice Corvette engine put beneath the hood. When John finished rebuilding the car, it was a powerful machine made for the racetrack or the open road. In fact, everyone who saw the car wanted to race it.

The bright color and the obvious power of this car drew eyes, but then John began to add the pictures and the autographs began to appear. As Trish related, they had a sign company put "Resistance Is Futile" on the rear of the car and wherever they went in the car, they would draw a crowd.

SEVENUVNINE IS KIDNAPPED

It is interesting that throughout the telling of her story, Trish referred to Sevenuvnine as another female, and yet, as so often happens, she clearly was not jealous of this other woman who was getting so much of her husband's time. In fact, she came to look at Sevenuvnine with as much affection as John.

They were both proud of the beauty that had appeared from beneath the drab gray paint that had originally covered the car. The tender loving care that was showered on the car had created a one of a kind symbol, but there are always the lazy and the worthless scum that populate the world and envy those who rise through hard work and dedication. What John and Trish had not counted on was that evil eyes were watching them and envied them their beautiful car.

As has been earlier in the story, for a long time **Sevenuvnine** was John's primary transportation and they also drove the car to the Conventions. Several years ago, they were living in Clairmont, Oklahoma and one evening they drove into Tulsa to go to the movies. Like any young couple John and Trish had only thoughts of an enjoyable evening on their mine. Nothing prepared them for one of the most traumatic nights of their life.

The movie was enjoyable and the popcorn and soda hit the spot. After a hard week, this was just what they needed in order to relax. Slowly, they made their way toward the exit, with a long drive home before them. However, when they came out of the theatre, they could not immediately spot their bright yellow car in the well-lit parking lot. Certain

---

[79] At no time did she take advantage of her involvement in this book to make any statement remotely critical of John for not listening to her. This makes her, in my mind, a very unusual woman. John is very lucky to have found her.

that they had just walked to the wrong are of the lot, they searched it again, and again. Finally, they came to the inescapable conclusion that the car was gone. Someone had stolen **Sevenuvnine**. John was devastated and they searched the parking lot and the surrounding area several times before giving up and calling the Police.

For the next five days, they searched high and low for this car that had become a part of their lives. Just as they would for a missing child or a lost pet, they made fliers and drove into Tulsa to post the fliers every place that they could think to put them. There was never a thought in their minds that they would not eventually get **Sevenuvnine** back. They had no basis for believing that they would be able to recover this unusual car, they just had faith.

As sometimes happen, their faith was rewarded, after five days, the

Figure 82: Crewmembers needing a shuttle ride back to the Enterprise?

Tulsa police called and reported that they had found the car. The Police had towed the car to the impound lot and they could come and get it. John and Trish literally burned up the road getting to Tulsa and their precious car. **Sevenuvnine** was coming home.

They were so happy to get **Sevenuvnine** back that it didn't matter to them that she was somewhat the worse for wear. The door locks had been broken and it had been driven hard, but surprisingly, it was in relatively good sense. In short order, they had her put back together than she looked better than ever.

As **Sevenuvnine** began to come into her own, she drew a lot of attention. Wherever John and Trish went in their unusual car, they would draw large crowds and people crowded around in order to read the autographs and inscriptions that covered the shining surface of the car.

At first, after having recovered **Sevenuvnine**, John and Trish were on their guard to ensure that she was not stolen again. However, as time passed, as is normally the case, they lowered their guard, not dreaming that the lazy and those always looking for a quick buck was watching with envy from a distance. A year after the car was stolen the first time, a second attempt was made to steal the Star Trek car. This time, though a window was knocked out, the thieves were interrupted and unable to make off with their prize.

Deciding that it was time to move to greener pastures, a year after this second attempt to steal **Sevenuvnine,** John and Trish moved to Fayetteville, Arkansas. **Sevenuvnine** was still used being as primary transportation when it was not being shown at Star Trek Conventions. Trish was fascinated at the crowds that would gather whenever they would drive down the street in the Star Trek car.

Every time they would walk away from the car, when they would return, there would be people gathered around the car looking at the pictures and autographs in complete fascination.

THE FIRST CONVENTION

Trish remembers the first convention that they ever attended as exhibitors and not as fans like it had happened yesterday. This first convention was held in Fayetteville, Arkansas and it was either the second or third year that the promoters had held a Star Trek Convention in Fayetteville. At this first convention, they parked **Sevenuvnine** beneath an awning type thing because it was cold and rainy that day. But in spite of all of the problems, they were finally at a convention.

It was at this first convention that they met Chase Masterson and Robert Picardo. Both of these stars happily signed **Sevenuvnine** and Trish found them to be warm, lovely people. She had some very good memories of this first convention as a result of her association with some of the stars.

THE NEXT CONVENTIONS

The next year, they again attended the Star Trek Convention in Fayetteville, Arkansas. Though this was not one of the major conventions held around the country each year, it was still important to the fans in Fayetteville and to John and Trish, since it was now their hometown.

This time they were give a much better location in which to display **Sevenuvnine** and they received much more fan attention and acceptance by the Stars than they had received the previous year. The fan response was just overwhelming, with many of them spending a great deal of time ogling the beautiful Star Trek Car. It was also at this convention that Trish first met Vaughn Armstrong, a man who would introduce she and John further into the world behind the scenes. Vaughn is a man that both John and Trish have described as a really wonderful man that treats you no different than he treats anyone else. He is both a well known

Figure 83: Nichelle Nichols signs

star and a true gentleman who has not forgotten where he came from.

The next convention that they attended was the one in Tulsa, Oklahoma in 2003. She described this convention as a very good one for she and John. Everybody wanted to see the Star Trek Car, walk around it and have their pictures taken with **Sevenuvnine** and John. It was also at this convention that both of them began to feel that they were getting close to accomplishing the dream that had been John's from childhood.

Due to the success that they have achieved with *Computer Solutions*, their company in Fayetteville, Arkansas, **Sevenuvnine** is no longer used as a primary means of transportation. Now the car is only brought out for display at the various conventions. **Sevenuvnine** is truly priceless, not only as a symbol of the Star Trek idea, but also because some of those who have signed **Sevenuvnine** have passed on their signatures can never be replaced. Not only John and Trish

Figure 84: Actor Casey Biggs

but also the many thousands of fans that flock to the conventions wanting to see the Star Trek car would be devastated if something happened to this car.

TWO MASTERPIECES

A lot of time, effort, and money has gone into creating **Sevenuvnine** and getting her to where she is today. The amazing Star Trek Car has not only been a consuming passion for John and Trish, but there have many others that have helped carry the dream forward. This effort would be almost impossible to repeat; truly this masterpiece could never be duplicated. It would be like trying to copy a Rembrandt or the work of Michelangelo.

What is as amazing and irreplaceable as **Sevenuvnine** has been the love and support that Trish has given to John and the complete and total support that she has given his dream of creating the first Star Trek Car. Trish is pleased at the total dedication that John has shown in his efforts to make his dream come true. She loves Star Trek, but she is nowhere as immersed in this make believe world of science fiction, as is John. He has lavished thousands of hours of his time and tens of thousands of their dollars creating **Sevenuvnine**. There are not many wives would stand by and watch so much money go into a project that literally has not returned on red cent of revenue. This is a very rare young lady.

THE REACTIONS

Figure 85: Actress Denise Crosby

Trish discussed at some length, the reaction of people when they take **Sevenuvnine** to a Star Trek Convention. The fans are just stunned at the beauty of the car and the autographs that cover the body. They spend a great deal of time reading the car and openly express their excitement at seeing the autographs of their favorite actors. Many of them even remain in the general area of the car, knowing that eventually the stars present at the events will come over the Sevenuvnine. But the really amazing reactions come from the actors themselves.

Many of the stars, when asked to sign the car, are very matter of fact about agreeing[80]. Some express some puzzlement at being asked to sign a car, or, like Kevin Sorbo, think they have to go out to the parking lot, but for the most part they agree. However, when they stars approach the car and see exactly what covers if from front to rear, generally their mouths drop open and many of them just stand amazed. In some of these famous personalities, the kid in them emerges and, just like the many fans, they walk around the car, reading the autographs, inscriptions and looking at all of the mementoes that others before them have left. Most of them have never been asked to sign a car before and it is really fun to watch their faces as they actually sign **Sevenuvnine.**

Trish is very grateful to John Harper of StarBase 21 for believing in John and **Sevenuvnine.** He gave them a chance to show this car to the fans, the stars, and the world in general. Without John Harper's support, the dream would have died almost stillborn. John Mercer has worked so hard to make **Sevenuvnine** what she is today and with John Harper's assistance, all of his hard work, pain, and suffering has paid off. More and more people have heard of the amazing Star Trek car and there are many fans that come to each convention to see what new autographs are on **Sevenuvnine.** She is a truly beautiful car, she has some flaws, but as Trish says, she is who she is! Flaws and all, she is an important part of their family.

There is only one thing that is needed to make **Sevenuvnine** complete and there is Jeri Ryan's autograph on **Sevenuvnine.** She was part of the inspiration for the creation of **Sevenuvnine** as she is today, the car is named after a character she portrayed and hers is one of the few autographs that he lacks. When he finally get Jeri's autograph, **Sevenuvnine** will finally be complete.

---

[80] Some for a price, of course.

Figure 86: Klingons feel that it is a treaty violation that there is no Klingon Interstellar Shuttle!

CHAPTER SIXTEEN

JOHN MERCER

In the telling of the saga of Sevenuvnine, there has naturally been some jumping around as other incidents are remembered that really should be included. After all, this is being done from memory and it is almost impossible to tell a story this involved and not repeat of have to back track to cover so essential details.

<u>SOME OBSERVATIONS</u>

One of the sad things that John has noticed is how some of the promoters and stars react to the fans. Promoting and running a major Star Trek Convention is a very expensive, time consuming and enjoyable undertaking. During his time being involved in the Convention world, John has noticed that some promoters do it for the community and the joy that an event such as a Star Trek Convention will bring to the fans, some promoters do it for the fun of interacting with the stars and socializing with other serious collectors, some promoters hold a Convention for the fans and some promoters do it just strictly for the money because a major successful convention can bring in an unbelievable amount of money.

Unfortunately, it seems that in many instances, we have gotten away from the holding of a Star Trek Convention merely for the love of the idea. This love, which in some cases can approach a true passion is what the fan has for the Star Trek phenomenon. Now, more often than not, for the promoters, the exhibitors and the stars, it is all about, first and foremost, the money. This is not what Star Trek stands for in the mind of that fan that pays his or her money to get a chance to meet the their favorite star.

John made it very clear that he is not intending to direct these comments toward anyone in particular. However, there is a passion that people have toward Star Trek that has been viewed by many as a threat. There have been major efforts undertaken to kill the very idea of Star Trek in the media, even on television. In spite of these efforts, the idea that is

Figure 87: Some autographs on Sevenuvnine.

Star Trek survives and continues to flourish.

Even now the UPN Network is airing Star Trek: Enterprise but the ratings are not great. Even as the ratings drop, the network tries to push and save the show simply because there are so many fans who are fanatical about having Star Trek. The last survey showed that there were over four million Star Trek fans in the country. These fans spend a lot of money and it is these fans who actually generate the next generation of fans as the idea is passed from parents to children. The network recognizes the sheer amount of buying power that these four million plus fans represent. There will be Star Trek is some incarnation or other for the foreseeable future.

MOTIVATION

Gene Roddenberry understood, perhaps better than most, what motivated the Star Trek fan. The reason that a fan will go to a Star Trek Convention and spend $50.00 or $200.00 or $800.00 or a $1,000.00 dollars at a Convention held to commemorate a show that only lasted three seasons is that they have a passion and a love for the stars and the series. Unfortunately, some of the stars have lost the understanding of who made them what they are today. This is a very sad commentary for a series that has touched part of the human psyche.

There are some actors living today whose names have become household words as a result of the Star Trek fans. Sadly, some of these same actors have forgotten that it was not their efforts alone that got them where they are today, but the support of the fans. When these stars show up at a Star Trek Convention more concerned with how much they will make as a result of their appearance and less concerned about the fans that have come to see them, this cheapens the meaning of their appearance.

There are certain stars of some of the Star Trek series that charge a very great deal to make appearances at these conventions. Once they arrive, they agree to do nothing that does not put some more money in their pockets. These are the stars that have forgotten the fans that made them stars. Frankly, the fans should forget these stars.

Sometimes, it is not the stars that have forgotten the fans but their promoters. Once at a convention in Tulsa, Robert Picardo made an appearance as a surprise guest. Robert knew John and immediately greeted him by name. John wanted to take a picture of Robert Picardo with Sevenuvnine and Robert was very agreeable as he always enjoyed reading the car and talking to John. However, as Robert stepped forward his promoter stopped him and said that there would be no pictures taken unless $20.00 was paid. John did not have the $20.00 available with which to pay.

Now it should be pointed out that there are two different types of promoters involved at a Star Trek Convention. There is the promoter of the event, itself and then there are the promoters representing the individual stars. The event promoters are generally very pro-fans, however, quite often the promoters of the individual stars try to maximize the profits realized by the stars, because the payment received by the promoters is based on what the star makes. Thus in the mind of this particular promoter representing Robert Picardo, a free picture was money out of the promoter's pocket.

On the other hand, some promoters, like Lolita Fatjo, who promotes several Star Trek stars, such as Chase Masterson, Jeffrey Combs, Dominic Keeton and Trinneer Connor, knows John and knows that he is not making a cent off of Sevenuvnine. She goes out of her way to help him get the signatures of those stars she promotes. She understands that when one gives, they tend to get.

Dave Scott, of Slanted Fedora, wanted to charge John a large sum of money, like he does everyone else, to display Sevenuvnine at one of his events. John explained that he did not make any money off of the car as he does not sell pictures, autographs, books, or anything else. He just wants the fans to see the car. Scott's response was that maybe you should star selling something because he would not take part in one of Scott's events until he did.

In 2002, Dave Scott was the master of Ceremonies for a Convention where John was displaying **Sevenuvnine**. The event promoter convinced Dave Scott to at least drive out and see the car, as Scott wanted nothing to do with John, nor his car. The promoter urged Scott to help John as he said that Scott had the contacts to make the Star Trek Car a success.

Dave Scott and Slanted Fedora promotes the Star Trek Convention in Las Vegas and for the first two years he was taking part in Conventions, John would call and ask to be included. However, he was told that unless he paid an exhibitor fee, he would not participate. In actuality, if he had the money to pay the promoter, John could take Sevenuvnine to any convention in the country. However, when he would say he did not have the money, he would be told that they were sold out and had no space to put a car. After he began to achieve some notice, then Dave Scott called and wanted John to take part in a Star Trek Convention in Little Rock, Arkansas.

WHERE DOES IT END?

At every show, John is asked when he will have completed his project. In his mind, the car can never be completed until Jeri Ryan puts her autograph on Sevenuvnine. She was the impetus for the beginning of the project and she will be the signal that the project has ended.

Unfortunately, he has no way to contact this lovely star and her promoter will not let John and Sevenuvnine get within a hundred miles of this young lady. Even if he takes the car to Los Angeles, how does he get word to her than he would like her to sign the car? Of course, there are some other star autographs that he needs, but Jeri Ryan's is the Holy Grail of the Sevenuvnine project. How does one win through to the Holy Grail?

John would like to have a permanent home for his baby. To John this car is not a mechanical device, but a person with a personality of its own. He drives her now only at events, from where the car is off loaded form the trailer to where she is to be parked for the exhibit. However, even so, he has a rapport that is absolutely uncanny. If she needs something, such as a tune up, or an oil change or there is something wrong, John knows it almost instinctively. So he feels this need that she has developed over the years for a permanent home.

If Gene Roddenberry, Jr. or Paramount created a museum for Star Trek and placed Sevenuvnine on display, John is sure that a call form them would get through to Jeri Ryan. An autograph is not too much to ask for a symbol that will last long after we are all dust and memories. If there were such a place created, John would donate the car in a heartbeat.

ACHIEVING THE IMPOSSLBLE

Against unbelievable odds, John has created the Star Trek car. He now has over 100 autographs on the car. He accomplished the unbelievable feat with few resources. He is not rich, nor famous; he is just an ordinary guy who gets up each morning and goes to work. Many people had told him that what he wanted to do was impossible, but John Mercer believed. This young man set himself a goal and no matter how hard the going has become, nor how many people laughed at him, he never lost his faith that he would complete the project. With money, his project would have been easy, but without money, it was unbelievably hard.

John views himself as a fan who happens to be on the inside. He is a guy who, every Wednesday night watches *Star Trek: Enterprise*, he buys the DVDs, he goes to the Conventions, he buys the books and collectibles. He has created the ultimate collectible, Sevenuvnine, but he does not make a dime off of this remarkable machine. His love for Star Trek and everything that the series stands for is visible for the world to see.

In the last five years he has met thousands of people at the various Star Trek Conventions that he has attended. He has met wealthy bankers and very successful business leaders as well as hourly menial laborers who were joined by their common love of Star Trek. On the floor of a Star Trek Convention there are just fans, there are no class distinctions. The fans of the Star Trek phenomenon cover the entire spectrum.

John, himself, is looked at by the fans as someone important, a star, of sorts in his own right. But in his mind, he is a common ordinary guy who just happens to be lucky to have access to the stars. He has been asked many times how one gets to where John has gotten. To them, and too all Star Trek fans, he says if you want to achieve the impossible, then you simply believe that it is not impossible. John is the living proof that what he says is true.

GOALS

In achieving his ultimate dream, John Mercer has settled on four goals. The first, of course was creating the Star Trek car. He has accomplished that. True he still needs some autographs to complete his project, but in the minds of the fans, he has succeeded. Of course, no one has any idea, until this book, how difficult accomplishing this goal would turn out to be.

His second goal is to have Jeri Lynn Ryan autograph Sevenuvnine.

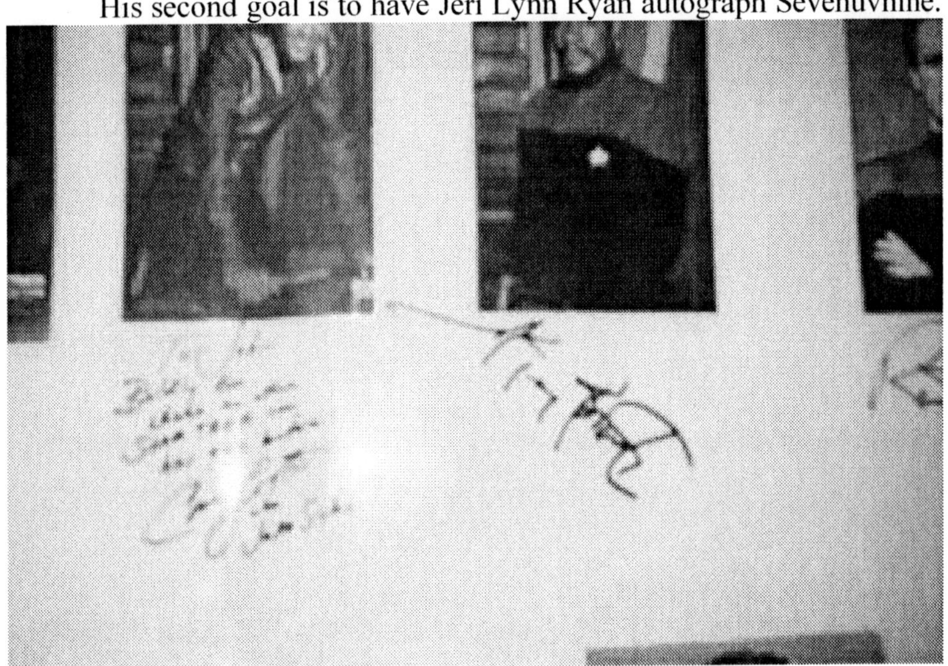

Figure 88: More autographs from Sevenuvnine.

Unfortunately, this goal is much harder than merely creating the Star Trek car. The last Convention where she was schedule to appear was in Texas. John was all set to go to this convention to see his favorite star when the promoter cancelled the event without any explanation. Now that she has achieved a regular's status on a new television series, she no longer

Figure 89: Cirroc Lofton has not forgotten the fans.

does any Star Trek Conventions. Additionally, her promoter is dead set on keeping John away from his star. So this goal may take a little longer to accomplish. However, how can a mere promoter stand between the man that single handedly created the Star Trek car based only on his drive, dedication, and sheer faith and his goal? My money is on John!

John's third goal in life is to create, or convince someone to create a permanent home for the most unique car in the world. This would insure that his achievement is displayed for the world to see. Sevenuvnine is a unique symbol of Star Trek. It can never be duplicated.

However, his ultimate goal would be a walk on role on Star Trek, playing a part with his own face. He is not an actor and does not want to be an actor, but to John, a walk on part on an episode of Star Trek would be the ultimate Star Trek collectible. He knows that he hasn't paid his dues to act. He hasn't studied and he hasn't taken all of the classes that many of them have taken, but, just as he can sing, he can act. All he needs is what the star received, a break.

Stars are people who have merely had breaks the rest of us never

Figure 90:Robert McNeil autographs Sevenuvnine.

had the opportunity to receive. When the idea of writing this book about Sevenuvnine was first raised in El Paso, the idea was in the back of his mind that perhaps this book might be the final assist that John needs to achieve this last goal. Only time will tell. He has made friends of many stars who said if it was their choice he would have a walk on role. But it is not what you know that makes these things happen, but rather who you know.

Finally, his ultimate dream and the act that would complete the Star Trek car would be the opportunity to meet the beautiful Jeri Ryan, the impetus for Sevenuvnine. He had one chance at a Star Trek convention in Texas, but at the last moment, her appearance was cancelled by the promoter. Now that she has started her series, she just simply does not make appearances any longer. So it is that even though he has not accomplished every one of his goals, very few people ridicule Sevenuvnine and John any more.

OUT TO PASTURE

Sevenuvnine is a powerful automobile built for the open road. However, John no longer drives this unique car, except for an occasional trip to the gas station or to a auto body shop. First the car insurance is expensive, how would you insure something like Sevenuvnine? It is also dangerous to drive this car. Oh, the danger is not for John as much as it is for other drivers. So Sevenuvnine spends most days sitting in an enclosed area, dreaming of exploring the galaxy, if cars have dreams. She lives vicariously through others as a result of her involvement at the Conventions.

CHAPTER SEVENTEEN

THE PROCESS

Figure 91: Sevenuvnine and "friend."

Some of the most frequent questions that John is asked at a Convention are "how do you get the photos on the car?" and "how do you keep the autographs from wearing off?" So John felt that these questions should be addressed in this book. After all, these issues are certainly part of the saga of **Sevenuvnine**.

BEFORE THE CONVENTION

When he decides what Conventions to attend, a decision usually based strictly on his finances, John must then decide what new pictures to mount on Sevenuvnine. At this point it should be understood that the Promoters of a Convention do not cover the complete cost of getting Sevenuvnine to come to the Convention (though the Promoters of the El Paso Convention came very close). John's expenses begin with the decision of what photos to add to the car.

First he must obtain the photos that he wants to include on the car and then have a sign company reproduce the picture on a special material called pleather[81], a manmade leather. Once the photo is UV coated, it will not fade and it is very difficult to damage. Some of the pictures on Sevenuvnine are four and five years old, and yet they look as new as they day they were placed on the car.

After the photo is prepared for mounting, John must decide where he wants to permanent mount the picture. The selected are is then sanded with 1200 grit fine sandpaper. After the area has been carefully sanded, the picture is mounted and then the picture, itself, must be carefully sanded with the 1200 grit fine sandpaper[82]. Once the picture has been sanded to John's satisfaction, he takes a bottle of plain water, adds a few drops of Dawn Dish Washing Soap, and then sprays the sanded photo. Carefully, he squeegees out any air bubbles and makes sure the photos is as flat as possible. Then the car is set out in the sun to bake. For this process to work correctly, the outside temperature must be between 75 – 80 degrees.

---

[81] Pleather is a polyurethane film that has been used for years by designers to mimic the properties of real leather. Pleather now represents the most daring and cutting edge textile usage available and is a predominant fabric in spring clothing lines by such designers as Gucci, Moschino, Prada, FUBU and Sean John.

Pleather's popularity has increased quickly due to its less expensive price, ease of care, and versatility. The cost of Pleather is three times less than its true leather counterpart. Pleather can also be cleaned easily as it can be wiped off with a mild detergent and a warm cloth. By placing the photos on a Pleather backing, the sign company can be sure that the picture will not wear off or be damaged by being placed on the body of the car.

[82] One of the benefits of the pleather material is that it lends itself to being sanded without damaging the picture. A Polaroid picture would be utterly destroyed if treated in this fashion.

After the car has baked in the sun and the new photo is dry and smooth, John then takes the same type of clear base coat that a dealer places on a new car and sprays the area of the new photo. In order for the photo to completely blend in with all of the older photos already in place, a very large body area much be sprayed. Once the first coat dries, then a second coat must be added. If three new photos are being added to the car, this can result in the need to clear complete the entire car at a cost of approximately $1,500.00.

This clear coat process is not without risks to the car, however. Sometimes, in the spraying of the new layer of clear coat, damage can occur. For this reason, a lot of auto body shops refuse to work on **Sevenuvnine** for the fear of potential liability.

<u>AFTER THE CONVENTION</u>

Once the star or stars has signed the car, then the clear coat process must be done all over again[83], or the autograph or inscription will fade over time, or even worse, smear. There was a reference earlier in the book

Figure 92: Armin Shimmerman signing Sevenuvnine.

---

[83] Each layer of clear coat costs approximately $1,500.00. Therefore each appearance at a convention costs John at least $3,000.00 for the before and after coats of clear coat.

a bout Ethan Phillips having to sign **Sevenuvnine** twice due to his autograph disappearing from the car and one Astronaut, Rick, who flew on the Space Shuttle, has his autograph smear. In the name of realism, John has left the smeared signature just as it is, but Ethan Phillips's autograph was replaced.

There is no question that most people do not understand exactly what has gone into creating Sevenuvnine. At on Las Vegas Star Trek Convention, a fan came over and examined Sevenuvnine from front to rear. Finally, he walked over to John and remarked that the car was beautiful, but it had some serious flaws. He recommended that the car be sanded down to the base metal and then repainted. Once the repainting was completed then the photos could be added once again and the stars all sign the car once more.

To John the very idea of sanding Sevenuvnine down to the base metal was horrifying. He is the first to admit that the car has some flaws, but she is what she is.

The concept of potential liability for a body shop actually stems from the adding of the clear coat once the autographs are on the car. Originally, John would buy paint pens containing enamel paint, very similar to the paint found in spray cans. The stars would use these paint pens to sign their autographs. However, sometimes when the clear coat would be added, the autograph would simply fade away. There are only a few body shops that are sure enough of their work to want to take the risk. Even if the clear coat causes the autographs to fade, the cost of the clear coat is still an additional $1,500.00.

HOW MUCH IS IT WORTH?

Another problem that John has run into is in insuring the vehicle. It is very hard to find a company that would insure the care for more than its replacement value as a car. Who is even qualified to appraise such a unique item?

As a car, replacement value might be only $1,000.00[84], but as the one and only Star Trek car, it is priceless. There is really no standard by which to gauge its true value. John has been offered some astronomical sums for the car, money that he has desperately needed, but he has not wanted to sell what he and his wife have come to look at as a member of

---

[84] Based on Blue Book value.

the family. He does, however, have hopes that if the car is eventually placed in a museum, the museum will offer him some financial compensation as well as notoriety for his hard work.

Though no one really knows the value of **Sevenuvnine**, everyone agrees that it is irreplaceable. Therefore, John does no more shows where **Sevenuvnine** cannot be displayed inside. If the car cannot be placed inside a building, then John declines the invitation to show the car. First and foremost, this decision is because he does not want to car exposed to the weather, but more importantly, if he is inside with the car, then the Stars will eventually walk up to him and he can ask them to autograph the car.

FAN INVOLVEMENT

The fans have been a major help to John in achieving his dream. For example, since John does not have anyone assisting him in exhibiting **Sevenuvnine**, he has no one to take photographs while he talks with the star about signing the car. This can cause a problem when it comes to authenticating the validity of a signature. He did not have a photo of William Shatner signing **Sevenuvnine**, but a fan sent him one. It is this fan involvement that has led John to feel that the car belongs to the fans as much as it does to him. The fans are one of the main reasons that **Sevenuvnine** exists. Without them, there would have been no way that John could have gotten the car to this point.

Chris Dunavan of Fayetteville, Arkansas, is a good friend to John and the head of the Fayetteville ship of StarFleet[85]. As a result of Chris's involvement, John and Sevenuvnine have been invited to come to the StarFleet Summit for Star Fleet Command in 2005. A Summit is a miniature convention where a number of stars come meet their more enthusiastic fans. As with all conventions, if not for the volunteers at a convention who are charged with making sure the star's needs are met the car would never happened.

NEGATIVES THAT BECOME POSITIVES

There is a negative side to the conventions that John has managed to turn into a plus. When he first began attending conventions and tried to

---

[85]StarFleet is a group formed of and for Star Trek Fans in 1974. This international organization, with a membership numbering over 4,000, is united in their appreciation of Star Trek: The Greatest Human Adventure. There are hundreds of chapters worldwide that link members into local happenings as well as the international organization.

get the stars to sign his car, he would sometimes have to stand for hours waiting for the star, fretting about whether the star would agree to sign Sevenuvnine.

This tedious part of the saga has actually become part of the legend of Sevenuvnine. When he is at a convention he has a number of people come up and ask him how he gets the signatures of the stars. He explains the lengths to which he has gone to get the many signatures that adorn the bright yellow car. He has become friends with many of the volunteers and these volunteers have worked long and hard to try and help John achieve his dream. As they escort their charges about the convention, the Volunteers try to get the stars to come over and sign the car.

However, for some stars, they have no earthly idea what the volunteer is talking about, thinking that the volunteer wants them to go to the parking lot and sign a car. This can sometimes be frustrating for the volunteer as well as the star, but without the volunteers, it is hard to get the star over to the booth, where Sevenuvnine is parked.

Then when he did the Star Trek Convention at Tulsa, John Harper was short handed and asked John if he would mind overseeing the photo shoot. Now normally, being asked to run such a large operation would have made it impossible for him to get the signatures that he seeks. However, it was immediately clear to John that being over the photo shoot meant that the stars would come to him and this would give him the chance to let them see Sevenuvnine and ask them to autograph the car.

He asked Chris Dunavan, a software expert and a good friend, to help him conduct the photo shoots. He told Chris that he and John Harper could split the money that the fans paid to have their pictures taken with the stars. When Chris objected as this act of benevolence on John's part, John told him he just wanted to autographs on the car. Finally it was agreed that if Jon had to pay for an autograph, Chris would reimbursement him from the photo funds. Otherwise, Chris and John Harper split the money. The photo shoot as run by John Mercer was so lucrative and efficient that he now has that assignment every year at the Tulsa Convention.

NEGATIVE ENERGY

When John was at the 2001 Star Trek Convention in Tulsa, OK, he had about 20 or 25 autographs on Sevenuvnine. This man walks up, sees all of the photos and autographs on the car and then turns, and looks at

John for quite some time before he says anything. Finally he asks what this car is doing here; then he remarks that this is a complete joke and a waste of time. Of course, these remarks hurt John feelings, but he stays calm and responds that this is his hobby and that everyone needs a hobby.

Not content at voicing his opinion, the man then demands to know how John can prove that he did not fake the signatures on the car, or trace the signatures. He sarcastically continued that John could have faked the entire car just to get into the convention for free and get to meet the stars. It was at this point that John first realized that he really did need a photographic record of each star as they signed the car in order to prove that their signatures were real.

In some cases, John did not personally have photos of some stars as they signed the car, but there are at least several thousand star trek fans over the career of Sevenuvnine who have each witnessed at least two stars sign the car and have pictures of the signings.

TREKKIES II

Denise Crosby is coming out with Trekkies II and Sevenuvnine was scheduled to e a part of it. When the filming of the Star Trek car was completed at his hours, for the movie, he called the promoters and asked if the 14 or 15 minutes of film would be enough for their purposes. He was told that that amount of footage would be sufficient because they were focusing on the odd things that Trekkies do overseas.

The point of the movie was to show the unusual or odd things that people did to commemorate Star Trek, such as designing the interior of their house to look like a star ship's bridge. John thought that this was odd because Sevenuvnine was certainly one of the more unusual items created by a Trekkie and there was a man in Fayetteville who went to work every day at a business called Sir Speedys in a Star Trek uniform. He would have thought that these things would have been important to the promoters, but apparently they had a different idea.

Up until the El Paso Convention, John had never offered an 8 x 10 photo of the car before. He decided with the El Paso Convention to make an attempt for the car to help pay its own way. John felt that he had gotten the car to the point where it should be able to carry itself. As a test, he provided autographed 8 x 10 photos and sold 40. However, he actually gave away more than he sold.

He quickly realized that there were a lot of fans in El Paso who would dearly love to have pictures of the car, but who were unable to afford to pay for them. It was not so long ago that John had been in that same position, so he turned away no one. Even with the many free ones he gave away, he realized enough income to pay for the fuel to bring Sevenuvnine to El Paso.

WHY A BOOK?

There will be many people who ask why a book is written about the Star Trek Car. The answer to that question is very simple. The purpose of the book is to share with people the road he traveled to create Sevenuvnine and to hopefully generate revenue so that the car can do more shows. John would like to take Sevenuvnine to every show in the United States and Canada and perhaps later, across the world.

If he should be asked to come display Sevenuvnine in Europe, there is no way that he would be able to afford to load the car onto a C134 and fly it anywhere. The cost would be just too much for him to afford. However, with a book, there is the possibility that there could be enough sales to defray at least part of the cost of transporting the car overseas. John and Sevenuvnine have already shown that they are able to accomplish the impossible, so who knows?

ONE LAST PLEA

John Mercer has one last request to make of those of you who are reading (or in the case of the audio book version) listening to this saga. If you are someone of means and have a love of Star Trek or if you have connections to Paramount, help John arrange for a permanent home for his child. Even the cost of storage is a heavy burden for a man of modest means such as John Mercer.

With a permanent home, the Star Trek car will be a visible symbol of Star Trek long after we have all gone to explore the mysteries of the universe, leaving others to carry on after us.

CHAPTER EIGHTEEN

THAT'S A WRAP

So there you have it, the story of one man's impossible dream and his struggle to make it come true. John Mercer believed and in his belief, he convinced others that his dream should be their dream. Together, they all created the one and only Star Trek car. A symbol that all things are possible!

MORE THAN A SHOW

I can't end this saga without telling one last story that John Mercer related in the preparation of this book. He came from a very dysfunctional family; in fact his mother was married fourteen times. John was alternately abused and ignored as he grew to manhood. As so many do who have never known a stable home, he joined the military. In fact, he served in the United States Marines and trained as a sniper. This activity allowed him to vent his aggression on others and was a channel for this anger.

However, along came the end of the cold war, President Clinton, and the peace dividend (not necessarily in that order). A lot of dedicated soldiers were told we don't need you anymore. John Mercer was one of these soldiers. The energy he had put into stalking his fellow man was now focused on achieving the dream of building the Star Trek Car. It is John's feeling that Trish Mercer and Sevenuvnine are what saved him from a wasted life. These two were his balance and his compass that enabled him to reach for the stars.

"LIVE LONG AND PROSPER!"

<u>WHERE SEVENUVNINE IS CONCERNED, ONE THING IS ABSOLUTELY CERTAIN!</u>

APPENDIX A

TELEVISION SERIES

Star Trek: The Original Series (1966)
Captain Christopher Pike – Jeffrey Hunter
Captain James T. Kirk – William Shatner
Mr. Spock – Leonard Nimoy
Dr. Leonard H. McCoy – Deforest Kelly
Lieutenant Uhura – Nichelle Nichols
Commander "Scotty" Scott – James Doohan
Lieutenant Sulu – George Takei
Ensign Chekov – Walter Koenig
Nurse Chapel - Majal Barrett Roddenberry

Star Trek: The Next Generation (1987)
Captain Jean Luc Picard – Patrick Stewart
Lieutenant Commander William Riker – Jonathan Frakes
Ships Counselor Deanna Troi – Marina Sirtis
Dr. Bevery Crusher – Gates McFadden
Wesley Crusher – Wil Wheaton
Lieutenant Commander Data – Brent Spiner
Tasha Yar – Denise Crosby
Lieutenant Commander Worf – Michael Dorn
Lieutenant Commander Geordi LaForge – LeVar Burton

Star Trek: Deep Space Nine (1992)
Captain Benjamin Sisko – Avery Brooks
Constable Odo – Rene Auberjonois
Lt. Ezri Dax – Nicole De Boer

Lt. Commander Worf - Michael Dorn
Lt. Commander Jadzie Dax – Terry Farrell
Jake Sisko – Cirroc Lofton
Chief Miles O'Brien – Colm Meaney
Quark – Armin Shimerman
Dr. Julian bashir – Alexander Siddig
Colonel Kira Nerys – Nana Visitor
Gul Dukat – March Alaimo
Damar – Casey Biggs
Weyoun/Brunt – Jeffrey Combs
Nog – Aron Eisenberg
Rom – Max Grodenchik
Chancellor Martok – John Hertzler
Elim Garak – Andrew Robinson

<u>Star Trek: Voyager (1995)</u>
Captain Kathryn Janeway – Kate Mulgrew
Chakotay – Robert Beltran
Holographic Doctor – Robert Picardo

<u>Star Trek: Enterprise (2001)</u>
Captain Jonathan Archer – Scott Bakula
Dr. Phlox – John Billingsley
SubCOmmander T-Pol – Jolene Blalock
Lieutenant Malcolm Reed - Dominic Keeting
Ensign Travis Mayweather - Anthony Montgomery
Ensigh Hoshi Sato - Linda Park
Commandr charles "Trip" Tucker III - Connor Trinneer

ANIMATED SERIES
Star Trek: The Animated Series (1973)

FEATURE FILMS

Star Trek: The Motion Picture (1979)

Star Trek II: The Wrath of Khan (1982)

Star Trek III: The Search for Spock (1984)

Star Trek IV: The Voyage Home (1986)

Star Trek V: The Final Frontier (1989)

Star Trek VI: The Undiscovered Country (1991)

Star Trek: Generations (1994)

Star Trek: Firest Contact (1996)

Star Trek: Insurrection (1998)

Star Trek: Nemesis (2002)

INDEX

I

J

K

L

M

N

O

Turnabout Intruder, 20

T

Printed in the United States
18931LVS00002B/241-273